D1632635

FATHER OF COMFORT

Other Kanaan Publications:

A FORETASTE OF HEAVEN (Autobiography)
BUILDING A WALL OF PRAYER
I WILL GIVE YOU THE TREASURES OF DARKNESS
ISRAEL, MY CHOSEN PEOPLE
MORE PRECIOUS THAN GOLD
NATURE OUT OF CONTROL?
REPENTANCE — THE JOY-FILLED LIFE
STRONG IN THE TIME OF TESTING
THE HIDDEN TREASURE IN SUFFERING
TURNING DEFEAT INTO VICTORY
YOURS IS THE VICTORY AND MAJESTY

Available in the UK from Christian bookshops.
        Trade orders: STL Freephone Bookline 0800 282728
        Bookfax 0800 282530

Available in the USA from:
        Evangelical Sisterhood of Mary
        P.O.Box 30022, Phoenix, AZ 85046-0022

Available in Canada from:
        Evangelical Sisterhood of Mary
        4285 Heritage Drive, Tracy, NB, E0G 3C0
and: R.R.1, Millet, Alberta, T0C 1Z0

Available in Australia from:
        Evangelical Sisterhood of Mary
        30 Taylor Place, Theresa Park, NSW 2570

Available in Germany from:
        Evangelical Sisterhood of Mary
        P.O.Box 13 01 29, D-64241 Darmstadt

FATHER OF COMFORT

Daily Reflections
on the God Who Cares

M. Basilea Schlink

KANAAN PUBLICATIONS
Evangelical Sisterhood of Mary
Darmstadt, Germany and Radlett, England

Contents

Foreword

God seems so remote, incomprehensible, unfathomable.
Then there is my life with all its earthly limitations, beset
with troubles and sorrows. Is it possible that these two
worlds could ever touch or merge? Many people today,
considering God to be irrelevant, turn to drink, drugs,
anything that will numb the pain, only to plunge into
even deeper misery.

Yet it is possible for God's world and ours to merge.
In fact, it is even possible to have very close contact with
Him: a personal relationship of love and childlike trust
in the Father. Amazingly, we become children of this
holy and seemingly remote God when we believe in Jesus
Christ, His only-begotten Son. In Him, God the Father
has drawn close to us; through His sacrificial death, God
the Father has granted us child status. Every day He
wants to reveal His fatherly love to us in a new and different way. This basic tenet of the Christian faith will
certainly be familiar to believers — at least theoretically
— but, no doubt, for many it needs to be rediscovered
and applied.

In an age of increasing instability, characterized by
'wars and rumours of wars', surely this is of special sig-
nificance. Only if we have learnt to trust the heavenly
Father, will we find the strength and courage to face the
greater testings ahead and experience His help. May
these short daily devotions assist us all in nurturing such
a trusting relationship.

January

January 1

You are in need of comfort. Then know there is Someone who has comfort ready for you. There is Someone who is deeply moved by all human suffering, including your own: God your Father. It is not difficult for Him to comfort you. His love is so great that He never fails to find words and ways to express comfort. And His power to help is so great that He always has a solution; it may not come right away, but it will be perfect in its timing.

January 2

A gracious proposal is being made to us. Not only may we receive the Father's love, forgiveness and goodness, but we may also give Him something in return – the fruit of glorifying Him before others, for when people see our good works they will give the Father glory and honour.

How will we respond to this gracious proposal? Will we thank the Father by seeking to bring Him joy? Will we allow God to prune our sinful nature so that our lives will be fruitful and produce those 'good works' pleasing to Him? That would be a true sign of gratitude to a Father who cannot bear to see anyone sad. *Matthew 5:16*

January 3

You wonder where your path will lead. You do not need to know. Just take the first step indicated by God. Then He will show you the next ... and the next ... Go step by step. One day you will realize that He has led you according to a wise plan along a path leading to a glorious goal.

January 4

God wants His wonder-working power and glory to be revealed before all the world. This happens through people who have faith in Him. He is waiting for this to happen through you too. There is a risk-taking element about faith. Dare to put your confidence in Him in a hopeless situation. Then you will be honouring God, bringing joy to His heart and magnifying His name in the sight of others. This in turn will enrich your life and make you happy, and the miracles you experience will strengthen your faith.

January 5

Trust in the goodness of the Father, even when His chastening hand is upon you and it hurts. At such times God is being especially fatherly and doing what is best for you. His wise and loving discipline prepares His children for heaven. Such love fitting you for heaven, where you will be happy for ever! In accepting discipline willingly, you can taste something of heaven's joy here and now.

January 6

God is love. He is merciful and abounding in loving-kindness. If you want to experience His mercy, be merciful to others. Then you will push open the door of His heart so that His mercy will flow over you.   *Matthew 5:7*

January 7

Which power is greater? Human power? Or the divine power of God, who has created all things? The logical answer must be: The Creator's power. So put your confidence in God, to whom everything is subject. Trust in His love. His power to help is stronger than all the powers of destruction.

January 8

Are you lacking anything? Someone is keeping a kindly eye on you and thinking of you. That 'Someone' is your loving Father in heaven. So do not be absorbed by yourself, your work or people. Turn instead to your Lord, who loves you and is waiting for you. Think about Him often. Speak with Him. Love Him. Thank Him. Then you will no longer be alone but will have the assurance of being united with Him. This union will strengthen and encourage you, and you will lack nothing.

January 9

In His infinite love God has prepared for us a precious gift: repentance. People living in repentance are spiritually richest. They continually experience the love, forgiveness and compassion of God. They have access to His heart and all the blessings of renewal. Those who turn from their sins, not just once, but daily, will experience abundant grace. God has promised grace to contrite, humble hearts – not to those who are self-righteous, overconfident and complacent. Reach out for repentance as something highly desirable. The love of God is holding it ready for you.

January 10

God calls Himself our Father in Jesus Christ. His primary concern is that we love Him, because a father wants to be loved by his children. We were created and redeemed to love God. Whoever loves God above all else has found his eternal destiny. In this life and the next he will experience deepest fulfilment and joy.

January 11

There is Someone who knows about our worries. He sees every anxious thought that crosses our minds. Knowing what pain anxiety causes, He wants to help. He promises to care for us. Could anything be better? He wants to deal with our worries; to smooth a path where we can no longer see one; to transform unbearable circumstances in His own way; and to send help. Cast your cares upon your heavenly Father. Thank Him in advance for sending help in your difficulties, and your heart will be filled with peace.

January 12

We have a heavenly Father who is almighty. The question is: Who will experience His mighty deeds? – Those who believe in His ability to do them. Faith is a power capable of transforming everything – not faith in a vacuum, but faith in the living Lord, who has power to help and who demonstrates this for those who trust in Him. Therefore, have faith in Him when you are in despair, and the storm will abate. Trust in Him when you are afraid, and your fears will be calmed. Believe, and you will experience miracles.

January 13

Do you find the burden God has laid upon you too heavy to bear? Perhaps the reason is that you do not bear it willingly step by step. Time and again you weigh it in your hands, wondering whether you can bear it at all. That way you never will. Such deliberations will just make you self-pitying – and the burden unbearable. Shoulder your cross willingly, and you will discover that you can bear it. It comes from the Father's hands. He has weighed it for you in love. So it can never be too heavy.

January 14

Creation declares that God alone is the Maker. This means that it is not we human beings who are the creators of the universe. We are creatures, not masters. We are dependent upon God. Where there is no love, however, there is no willingness to be dependent – only a desire to be free, to have one's own way and to be master of one's own destiny. But whoever loves rejoices in his dependence, just as a child is happy to be dependent upon his father. Dependence ties the bond of love even more tightly.

Accept this dependence upon God the Father as His child, and you will be a child of God in the truest sense of the word, experiencing the joy and benefits of this relationship. You will discover how blessed it is to be loved, guided and cared for by God the Father.

January 15

Let us be glad that we are being guided in this life. The hand of the Father is directing us according to a wise, eternal plan. Day by day His wisdom is leading us on. Do not oppose His guidance, otherwise you will destroy a most glorious plan for your life. Accept His will, even when it is hard for you to make any sense of it. Then your path will end in joy and bliss for eternity.

January 16

You have been let down by people in whom you had placed your hopes. You feel disappointed, especially if they are Christians. However, God has allowed this disappointment in your life for a purpose. Every hope you set in people is to come to naught, so that you put your hope and trust in God alone.

God is the only one who never disappoints us.

Somewhere along the line people will fail us, for they are fallible. Even the Church of Jesus Christ is only a lowly 'manger' into which the treasure of the Gospel has been laid. It is this treasure which you should seek. It will last for ever and never lose its worth. Rather, the more you know it, the more precious it will be – like our Lord Jesus Christ.

The love of God had a reason in sending you disappointment. Let it accomplish its purpose in your heart. Be all the more grateful that God never disappoints you. Turn to Him alone and love Him even more. And out of this love for God, learn to love those whom He loves – the failure, the sinner.

January 17

Once – perhaps it was only yesterday – you saw how God answered prayer, helped you in your troubles and brought you through your afflictions. Once – perhaps it was only yesterday – when you were very sad, you saw how He comforted you and did not allow you to be tempted beyond your powers of endurance.

Do you think that the God of yesterday is not the same as the God of today? Believe that just as 'Jesus Christ is the same yesterday and today and for ever', so is God your Father the same for all eternity. He will take care of you today as well. He will not allow you to be tempted beyond your powers of endurance today either, but will carry you through. Cling to this knowledge in implicit trust. Then you will overcome all difficulties through faith in the One whose power and love are the same today.   *Hebrews 13:8; 1 Corinthians 10:13*

January 18

Does the prospect of the use of nuclear weapons make
you afraid? How do you overcome this fear? – By filling
your thoughts with the love of God the Father. Whoever
considers His love will be comforted. God always finds a
way to help and protect, even in the greatest affliction.
For instance, He can command fire not to burn.
Remember the angel sent to help Daniel's friends in the
fiery furnace. God declares He will be with His children
in their distress – a promise valid for all times. He says,
'When you pass through the waters I will be with you;
and through the rivers, they shall not overwhelm you;
when you walk through fire you shall not be burned, and
the flame shall not consume you.' God will be near you
in times of acute distress and will help you. May this
comforting assurance sustain you.   *Isaiah 43:2*

January 19

God the Father loves us and wants to speak with us. He
wants to reveal Himself to us and to share His deepest
feelings with us. However, He is the Holy One. Meeting
God means taking one's shoes off, figuratively speaking.
It means withdrawing at certain times from people and
from things demanding our attention; leaving the hustle
and bustle of everyday life; becoming still inside, waiting
for God to speak. Those who do so will have encounters
with God which will change their lives and empower
them for service in His kingdom.

January 20

When we judge and lash out against people we find hard
to bear, we are actually lashing out against God Himself.
People who rub us up the wrong way are His instruments. God has sent them in His wise plan to make us

humble and teach us to love. So humble yourself beneath the loving hand of God. When others make life difficult for you, accept this as God's dealing, and you will experience the blessing God intends for you in this situation.

January 21

Our love is precious to God the Father. He values it highly. Time and again He calls us to love Him, promising to love us in return. He wants to make His home in our hearts. Yes, He wants to visit you if you love Him. What an unimaginable privilege and honour! Do not throw it away frivolously. Give God your love. You may ask how. Jesus gives you the answer: 'He who has my commandments and keeps them, he it is who loves me.' This is not a matter of feelings. It is simply a matter of obeying His commandments, above all, His commandment of love – love which does not become resentful but which bears and endures all things. Those who strive daily to keep His commandments will experience the Father's love most.   *John 14:21; 1 Corinthians 13*

January 22

People living in expectation are eager and happy. They are never bored. There is something exciting about waiting when it contains the element of love. Wait in this way for the coming of God your Father. He is coming, because His love continually draws Him to us. He always brings something wonderful with Him: a scripture, a joy, a present. Look out expectantly for Him, and new life and happiness will fill your heart.

January 23

'Sing to the Lord.' Even on days when there is so much to do? – Yes, precisely then. When we sing, heaven comes down. God draws close when we sing praises to Him. Then our activities will be under the guidance of His Spirit. And whatever we do will be successful, being under His blessing. We will receive the strength to overcome the difficulties that arise. Our work will yield eternal fruit, because it has been done in union with God.

Psalm 96:1

January 24

In all eternity the love of God the Father can never be fathomed. He has been hurt and insulted by us. Our sins brought immeasurable pain and death to His only-begotten Son. What is God's answer to our shameful conduct? God accepts us as His children through faith in Jesus Christ. He loves us tenderly and cares for us. He opens heaven for us so that we may one day enter into His glory.

And yet we dare to be ungrateful and proud. Unbelievably, we rebel against God time and again. We accuse Him when we do not understand His actions and leadings. We think that He is being hard on us. We should not be surprised, then, if our relationship with God is disrupted and we do not receive any help or comfort. God gives grace only to the humble.

January 25

A true child of the heavenly Father has a sense of wonder. He never ceases to be amazed at what the heavenly Father knows and can do and at the way He showers goodness upon him. Awe and reverence grow out of this sense of wonder. Those recognizing most clearly their limitations and helplessness will be those most able to worship God for His omnipotence, wisdom and love. Are we gripped with wonder when we consider the greatness, glory and love of God? Do we worship Him with awe and reverence? Do we bear this mark of a true child of God?

January 26
Pray daily in the words of the disciples, 'Increase our faith!' A strong faith is something we often lack. Yet in order to perform the tasks God gives, faith is essential. In all your work and activities, yes, even in your prayer life, everything depends on having faith. Faith determines whether your prayers and actions will be fruitful. You may offer many prayers to God, perhaps even repeating the same request again and again. However, if you do not count on God having help prepared, nor expect it to come, then nothing will happen. If you are lacking faith, ask for it and count on God answering. He will produce faith in you. Then, having blessed this first step of faith, God will inspire you with further prayers of faith.

Luke 17:5

January 27
God loves the small and lowly, who can accept correction. But God turns away from those who accuse others, either in their hearts or verbally. They bear the traits of the Accuser, proud Lucifer, the enemy of God. If you wish to be loved by God, be your own accuser. Do not take sides against others. Only take sides against yourself. Then God will be on your side. He will show you His love and will act on your behalf.

January 28
Written over Job's life are the words, 'The Lord is compassionate and merciful.' The Lord was filled with pity for Job. As the heavenly Father, God suffered with His

servant Job when he endured affliction. Whoever suffers with the sufferer will try to ensure a good outcome. This is why in the end God more than restored all that Job had lost. This is an eternal law of the love of God in dealing with His chosen ones. So wait for the gracious ending of your suffering, and you will find that God will grant you more blessings than before.   *James 5:11*

January 29

When times are turbulent and wars rage, rejoice that you may sit in the shelter of the Most High, in keeping with His promise. God has pledged Himself to prove His might on behalf of His children when they are suffering affliction or are traumatized by war. Thank Him. Great strength lies in giving thanks and rejoicing. You need that strength to cope with times of trouble and oppressive fears of the future. Strength, born of thanksgiving and rejoicing, will make you victorious.   *Psalm 91:1-2*

January 30

God has wonderfully blessed His children, giving not only natural eyes to see the visible but eyes of faith to see the invisible. What goes on in the spiritual realm determines the visible world. Whoever uses his eyes of faith will be able to recognize the mystery of the love of God at work in his own life and in human history.

Then we will see not only the trials and tribulations but the glory that suffering is preparing for us; not only our sin but the victory Jesus won and wants to establish in our lives; not only the tangled fates of others and of ourselves but the wise and wonderful plan of God behind it all; not only the darkness spreading over the earth but the dawning of Jesus' eternal kingdom. So look at the unseen, look at the great promises of God, and your life will be transformed.

January 31

You are about to give up. You feel you cannot keep up the struggle any longer. You think it is all pointless. However, God is love. With Him, nothing is in vain. This is what Calvary shows us. Here seeming defeat culminated in the most glorious victory. So God is challenging you not to give up the battle and lose, but to keep up the struggle and win. So take up the battle again, and you will triumph. The cross of Jesus is over you as the sign of victory.

February

February 1

You are troubled and anxious. Yet you cannot solve your problems and difficulties by yourself. Your own restless thoughts and aspirations are making you weak and incompetent. They clog the channel of your heart through which God wants His help to flow. Leave everything to God. Let all your restless thoughts, worrying and frenetic planning come to rest. Rest in God and in His sovereign rule in the knowledge that He will act. Then you will discover that 'in quietness and in trust shall be your strength'. So choose this course and you will experience help.   *Isaiah 30:15*

February 2

God Himself tells us that He delights in doing His children good. However, He often has to wait until we are ready to receive the good things; otherwise we would trample them underfoot, so to speak. First He has to prepare us so that we are able to receive His good gifts in the right spirit; only then will they bring us true joy and blessing. Instead of being defiant when having to wait, let us willingly accept God's chastening, which is preparing us to receive His good gifts properly. Then we will receive them more quickly. When God can grant His gifts partly depends on us.   *Jeremiah 32:41*

February 3

Because God is love, He yearns for the love of His children. But how do you show your love for Him? Love God by doing good to others, by loving them as yourself. Love God by emphatically saying no to every sin. Love

God by being reconciled with others, just as He reconciled Himself with you in His only-begotten Son. Love God by giving up your self-love and self-will. Love God, who constantly bestows His blessings upon you, by surrendering yourself with all that you are and have. He will richly repay your love.

February 4
Those in suffering, inner conflict, or distress because of their sins are the first to find their way back home to the heart of God. A child in tears belongs in the Father's arms – arms wide open to receive him.

February 5
Whoever wants to know what a loving Father we have in God should picture, in spirit, the City of God. Prompted by His love for us, God has prepared a heavenly creation full of glory and perfect beauty to be the eternal dwelling-place of those who belong to Him. The Father wants to see His children happy. That is why He has prepared heaven, the City of God, for their eternal home. In days of suffering think of the love of the Father, which has prepared for you a heaven of perfect happiness and glory. Then all earthly suffering will lose its power to make you sad.

February 6
It is often part of God's strategy to wait until our problems have reached a climax. That is how God acted with the disciples when a storm blew up on the lake and they were in great distress. God could have calmed the first wave that arose. But then the disciples would never have known the power and glory of Jesus Christ. Bear this in mind when the waves around you become higher and

higher. God purposely lets them rise so high: He wants to prove His glorious power, do miracles and glorify His name.

Wait for Him to reveal His glory and wonder-working power in your situation of need, and you will experience the truth of this verse: 'Did I not tell you that if you would believe you would see the glory of God?'

John 11:40

February 7

God is a true Father. It is part of His nature to admonish and discipline His children. In His love He cannot stand idly by while people rush headlong into disaster and ruin their lives now and eternally. If there is no other way to make them listen, He resorts to warnings and discipline, in order to save at least some. Listen to His rebukes, and you will be spared many disciplinary measures and blows of judgment.

February 8

You think that God is fighting against you. But trust that whenever God seems to be fighting against you, He is actually fighting for you. He is your loving Father and always will be. Only sometimes does He act as if He were an enemy – as He once did with Jacob – in order to challenge you to a persevering battle of faith. Like Jacob, you should constantly repeat, 'I will not let You go, unless You bless me.' God wants you to emerge victorious from such wrestling in faith. He wants to make you a channel of blessing, one to whom He can entrust great commissions.

Genesis 32

February 9

Living in the nuclear age, we seek security as no other generation. In the coming time of great distress only those who are already at home in the heart of God will be secure. Those who can say now amid trouble and anxiety, 'The Lord is good, a stronghold in the day of trouble,' will know the reality of this affirmation when faced with even greater trouble and anxiety. So let us use present difficulties to practise living in the security of His heart. Then we will be able to do the same in the time of testing.   *Nahum 1:7*

February 10

The heavenly Father always has joys in store for His children – not just in heaven but here and now. He wants to grant His children the hidden treasures of the kingdom of heaven. He wants to disclose to them the secret of heavenly, festive joy even in this life. Do not set the joys and pleasures of this world above the gifts of God, doubting that God will really give you true happiness and fulfilment here and now. When life grows dark and earthly joys grow dim, you will then be desperately poor. Dare to forgo earthly joys for the sake of heavenly, eternal joys. You will not regret it. Rather, you will experience the fullness of joy. Do not wait until the doors are closed before turning to your heavenly Father in complete confidence, otherwise it will be too late.

February 11

In whom does the heavenly Father take delight? Who is it that brings Him joy? It is the child who repents and returns to the Father daily, saying like the prodigal son, 'Father, I have sinned.' The Father's heart will be drawn to him in love, for He rejoices over every sinner who

repents. Be such a child of the Father, and His approval
will rest upon you.   *Luke 15:18*

February 12
In God's Word we read, 'My father and my mother have
forsaken me, but the Lord will take me up.' When
deprived of human assistance and support, we will experience God's power. A person who puts his trust in
crutches cannot be taught how to walk. This is why the
Lord challenges us in our hearts, 'Throw away your
crutches so that My power can be effective for you.
When you go your way in My strength, then victory and
joy will be yours. So stop imposing limitations on My
power.'   *Psalm 27:10*

February 13
You know that God is your Father. However, it seems as
though you no longer have access to Him. You think that
your failings are too great in the sight of God and man.
But God is challenging you simply to accept the fact that
you have failed. Saying 'Yes, I have failed' is being honest. It is a sign of courage and humility. This 'yes' is the
key that will unlock the Father's heart. A stream of grace
will be poured out on you. Admitting your failings will
also open the door to the hearts of those whom you have
wronged. What a gracious opportunity God is giving
you!

February 14
By His disciplinary measures God wants to rescue individuals and nations from the misery caused by their own
sin. The judgments of God are an appeal for people to
turn from paths of sin, so that they might experience
deliverance and salvation. Do not resist God's discipline.

Judgment carries with it a tremendous offer. For you, too, grace lies hidden in judgment.

February 15

God suffers as a Father, because so often people, including His own, ignore Him. All too frequently, when in need of help, the last one we turn to is the Lord. But whoever has not learnt to count on God and His very real help now in everyday life will not be able to do so in times of trouble either, when all human help fails. That person will see no way out. So it is important to learn to count on God's help today.

February 16

Jesus brings good news: Sinners, wretched human beings, may say Father to the omnipotent God who created a universe of glory and magnificence. Are you conscious of this wonderful benefit? Avail yourself of the privilege of having an all-powerful ruler for your Father. Make use of it through childlike, trusting prayer, and you will receive help when you need it.

February 17

As far as our lives are concerned, we are construction workers, not architects. We do not have to plan for our whole life. The Architect of our life, who holds the blueprint in His hands, is God Himself. We are not being tossed about by blind fate. God is leading us according to a marvellous plan, along a path best suited to our strengths and abilities.

Do not prevent God from being the Architect of your life. Desire to be and do what is fitting for you: be obedient to His leading and place the stones day by day according to His plan in the building of your life – and a wonderful edifice will come into being.

February 18

When you cannot shake off sadness and depression, say these words aloud, 'Yes, Father, I want my cross.' Saying this will ease your heavy burden. Acceptance of God's dealings transforms the human heart. Surrendering our will takes the sting out of hardship.

February 19

God calls Himself your Father. He is waiting for you, His child, to love Him. The Father is looking for your love, for He delights in the love of His children. But you will be a joy to Him only in so far as you love God above all else. This means surrendering to Him everything your heart clings to, be it people or things, giving Him your all for love of Him. Then you will bring joy to the heart of God and, in loving God and being loved by Him, you will be richly blessed and happy.

February 20

A nuclear war, with its accompanying fall-out, devastation and trauma, would be the end of everything – or so people conclude. Those who belong to God, however, have His promise of help even for such times: 'Our God is a God of salvation; and to God, the Lord, belongs escape from death.' As the Prince of Life, Jesus is stronger than all the powers of destruction and can rescue us from death in miraculous ways. But should He at such a time choose to call us home, He will lead us gently through the gate of death, for His very presence overcomes the power of death.   *Psalm 68:20*

February 21

Perhaps you are grumbling in your heart that God does not give you any comfort or help in your suffering. However, it is this very grumbling, your complaining against the burden of your cross, and your defiance of God's leading, that has erected a dam which in turn obstructs the flow of comfort and help He intends for you. Recommit yourself to God, wholeheartedly accepting His leading and His working in you. Then the way will be free for the blessing contained in suffering to flow into your life.

February 22

You are wondering how your problems can be solved. You have considered all the possibilities that meet the eye. However, the solution will come from somewhere completely different – from the unseen world, from God your Father. Count on God really being there. Then, all at once, you will sense His closeness and experience His help.

February 23

The Father in His love has planned an abundant reward for all His children's tears. He Himself wants to wipe away every tear from our eyes. Like the father of the prodigal, He wants to embrace us and shower us with love. After the troubles of this life He wants to give us an eternal weight of glory beyond all comparison. Rejoicing and gladness will take hold of us. He will repay us without end for our sufferings. Full of joy, He will show us the harvest of our days on earth. As we keep our thoughts focused on such a glorious outcome, our greatest suffering will seem small to us.

Revelation 21:4; 2 Corinthians 4:17

February 24

God is love! May this fact be sufficient for you. Do not try to understand God when His leadings seem to you unfathomable. Rather, humble yourself beneath them. Then you will become wise, and God's heart will be opened for you. Through humble love you will be able to comprehend deeply the nature of His love, even if your human reasoning still fails to fathom His actions. Humble yourself beneath the powerful hand of God and you will find peace. You will rest in His will amid all His incomprehensible leadings.

February 25

You know what it is to pray. But that is not enough. You need to pray in faith, firmly trusting in God's help. Put your faith into action. Do not just bring petitions. Pray like this: 'Thank You that You have already planned help for me. Thank You that You have a solution to my problem. Thank You that Jesus' victory over my sin has already been won.' There is a promise attached to such prayer. It moves the arm of God so that the difficulty must yield before His almighty power. Make use of this provision. Through thanksgiving you will become happy and strong. When your pleas to the heavenly Father are embedded in thanksgiving and faith, they will be heard.

Matthew 21:22; Philippians 4:6

February 26

What is God's ultimate goal for your life? God arranges everything in our lives in order to teach us to love. Through His only-begotten Son He has redeemed us so that we might reflect the most beautiful thing there is: divine love. Interpreting His leadings in this light is of special help when God brings difficult people into your life.

February 27

'I am lacking in this and that, in fact, in everything, and so there is no help for me' – or so you conclude. However, as far as God your Father is concerned, it makes no difference whether you lack much or little. On the contrary, the greater your needs, the more He can demonstrate His wonder-working power. Rejoice in the assurance: 'God will give me what I lack for the very reason that I am lacking so much.' Such faith will bring about a transformation of circumstances.

February 28

God loves us. This is why He longs for us to rejoice and be glad on the day of His Son's return. Who will experience this joy? – Those who suffer with Christ. However, this joy is not just reserved for the Second Coming. We are to experience it here and now during suffering, for in the name of God the apostle Peter challenges us to 'rejoice in so far as you share Christ's sufferings'. He even calls it a special privilege to suffer pain and disgrace for Jesus' sake. Why? It is the way to the abundant joy our heavenly Father wants to give. He cannot bear to see anyone sad.

When God counts you worthy of being misunderstood, excluded and humiliated for His name's sake, say, 'Thank You for counting me worthy of suffering for Your name's sake.' Then joy will enter your heart.

1 Peter 4:13

February 29

You have fallen down and made yourself dirty. You no longer dare to step into God's presence. He seems so remote. But it is exactly now that the Father is waiting for you. He waits for His child who has sinned, as a mother waits for her child who has fallen down and become dirty, so that she can wash him. He wants to cleanse you in the blood of His Son. So come.

March

March 1

God our heavenly Father is the one true Father, whose heart is nothing but goodness and love. Everyone who trusts in Him will experience this. But whoever doubts God, thinking that He does not want the best for us and that He will not help us, will receive no help. Mistrust destroys any loving relationship with the Father and ties His hands. We will have what our faith expects – and nothing more.

March 2

You say you have not received any comfort on your path of suffering. Is it perhaps because you are not bending down low enough beneath your cross? Perhaps you have not yet said with all your heart, 'I will gladly bear my cross, heavenly Father. I need it.' The prayer 'Yes, Father' contains great power. It will make your cross light for you. You will discover the Father's love in it. Therefore, say this one word 'yes', and you will receive comfort.

March 3

God knows our hearts. He knows that so often we are weak when it comes to trusting Him. This is why He gives us promises. These are valid. God does not disappoint His children, whom He loves. We have His promise, for instance, that in times of trouble He will protect those who acknowledge His name. Stand firmly upon His Word and take refuge in Him. Then you will find that His hand, which has created the world, is greater than nuclear power and the forces of nature,

stronger indeed than all other powers – and can hold
them in check.   *Psalm 91:14-15*

March 4

God is love. Thus it is His heart's desire that His children
learn to love. He knows that if we love, all will be well.
We can almost hear Him pleading, 'Love, as I have loved
you – love without seeking love in return. Bear with
those who do evil to you, as your Father bears with the
wicked. Return good for the evil done to you in word or
deed. Love others with a love that always thinks the best
of them and never grows weary but is prepared to bear
everything.'

This love is victorious. This love has power, because
it flows from God's heart into ours. May it be our most
fervent desire to attain this love. 'Ask, and you will
receive' is the Lord's promise to all.   *John 16:24*

March 5

Are you lacking faith? Your faith will be kindled when
you contemplate God's nature. Prayerfully pronounce
the attributes of God: 'You are almighty, all-wise, all-
loving, merciful, ever-present.' Say with Job, 'I know
that thou canst do all things, and that no purpose of
thine can be thwarted.' Or join Paul in praising God: 'O
the depth of the riches and wisdom and knowledge of
God! How unsearchable are his judgments and how
inscrutable his ways! From him and through him and to
him are all things.' Your faith will be kindled when you
proclaim the might and wisdom of God. Then you will
know from experience that those who believe in the
power of the almighty God never lack anything.

Job 42:2; Romans 11:33, 36

March 6

God has no option but to judge us, because He loves us. Yet, whenever He has to judge us, His compassionate heart weeps. Jesus wept when He spoke of the destruction of Jerusalem. The heart of God feels for us. He suffers with us when we suffer. It is hard for Him to discipline us. But how easy it is for us to make Him relent. When we turn from ways which grieve God and others, and when we begin to weep over our sins, Jesus' tears will cease and God's punishment will be turned into grace.

March 7

As the Father of love, God gives liberally. This we can see in the beauty He lavishes on nature and in the gifts and abilities He gives to His children. He is a rich giver. Are you perhaps poor because you have a small heart that does not expect anything big from Him?

March 8

Keep your quiet times with God. Give Him more time. There is no substitute for abiding in God's presence. In His presence you will become strong. Through being in His presence, you will be transformed. Seek His presence, and everything will be solved that you cannot solve by yourself.

March 9

The kingdom of heaven with all its blessings in the way of security, holy carefreeness, love and happiness belongs to children. However, being a child of God must be practised through lowliness and humility in everyday life. God's children ask people to forgive them. They humble themselves before others. They are willing to take the last place, to be counted as nothing. They accept correction from others like a little child. Those who do so experience the truth of the promise that the kingdom of heaven belongs to children. Here and now they have a foretaste of heaven.

Matthew 19:14

March 10

There are three little words that contain the answer to all your difficulties: 'Trust in God.' This means believing that God really is almighty and that He is a loving Father, always ready to help. Trust, and the first step towards the solution of your problems has been taken. The second will follow. You will see with your own eyes how in His time He will transform your sorrow into joy.

March 11

Do you want to know what the love of God your Father is like? Then listen to His words, 'I will remember their sin no more.' God forgets our sins, even the most grievous ones, if we show by our actions that we are truly sorry and turn from them. But there is something which He will never forget: the smallest deed and sacrifice inspired by love for Him. Who can fathom God's love? Knowing that He acts like this will give you the courage to trust His love in dark hours.

Jeremiah 31:34

March 12

Whoever has a wish goes to the one most likely to fulfil it: someone who loves him. No one loves you as much as God, who calls Himself your Father. Come to Him with your wishes. Come to Him like a child who pleads with his father until he fulfils his request. When we ask Him in a childlike and trusting manner with humble, obedient hearts, we will receive everything except what would be harmful for us. Be a child and, as a child, you will receive present after present from your heavenly Father.

March 13

One thing is certain for God's children in times of great distress: God the Father will stake His honour on living up to His name – the Almighty. He wants to demonstrate His power in our lives through miraculous instances of His help. At the height of trouble He will prove Himself greater than our plight. Wind and waves and the forces of destruction are subject to Him. He will wonderfully sustain His children, His chosen ones, who cry to Him day and night.   *Luke 18:7*

March 14

The heart of God our Father is brimming over with love. The Bible says that He wants to do far more for us than we ever dare ask or imagine. Indeed, we will be amazed at all the good He will do for us. He wants joy to well up in our hearts. This is why Jesus says, 'These things I have spoken to you … that your joy may be full.'

Do we believe that God wants to give us overflowing joy? Only then will we receive this joy, which will fill us with amazement – yes, awe and wonder – because of all the good things the Father in heaven does for us. Ask in the name of Jesus for this gift of joy which God has prepared for you. God is waiting for you to ask, so that He can fulfil your request.   *Ephesians 3:20; John 15:11*

March 15

Why do we so often become agitated, annoyed and anxious? By getting upset and worrying, we prevent God from working in our lives and blessing our activities. The root of our problem is self-will. We want things to go at our pace or in a specific way. Our will has not been surrendered to God.

Stop whenever you sense yourself becoming worked up. Be still before God. Commit your will to Him and say, 'I fully accept whatever You do, however You lead me, whatever You deny me. The way You arrange matters is always good. I trust You. I commit myself to Your will. Lord Jesus, You have redeemed me from my self-will and worrying.' Then you will sense the peace of God flowing into your heart, and your work will be blessed.

March 16

God, who is great and almighty, likes to do great things. But He seldom can, because we stand in His way with our own greatness, self-importance and overconfidence. This is why He appeals to us to humble ourselves and become small and lowly. He does great things only in the lives of the humble, who do not stand in His way.

March 17

Jesus teaches us to pray, 'Your will be done.' And this is to our advantage, for, with this plea, we exclude the possibility that our will is done. Because our will is limited and inclined to err, having our own way does not guarantee happiness. Indeed, it is more likely to have the opposite effect. But if God's will is done, then that is the will of perfect wisdom and of perfect love. We do not know what is good for us; only God does. So pray with the complete surrender of your will and desires, 'Your will be done.' In surrendering to His will unreservedly, you will have made the best choice for your life. The loving will of God will lead you to the supreme goal – the heavenly glory.

March 18

When you are sad and in distress, the heavenly Father asks you, as it were, 'Why are you cast down and feeling so discouraged? I have help in store. Wait and expect help. It will surely come. Yes, I tell you that one day you will give thanks with a joyful heart for that which is depressing you now.' Start praying, 'I thank You for the assurance that I can go forward confidently in expectation of help.' And you will proceed confidently, going forth to meet the day of help.

March 19

Paths of preparation and chastening are often the answer to our prayer to become more like Jesus and to receive from Him one day the unfading crown of glory. Now the Lord is leading you towards the desired goal. You would not reach it by following an easier route, otherwise God would have chosen that path. Lovingly accept God's leading, for ultimately it is the fulfilment of your prayer and will bring you the glory of heaven.

2 Corinthians 3:18; 1 Peter 5:4

March 20

You ask why God does not answer your prayers. It could be that there is some obstacle. For instance, if we misuse the gift of His forgiveness by not forgiving others, we block the way for further gifts of God. And so when God does not answer, you should first ask whether there is a prayer hindrance and what it might be. Let God show you what you have done wrong. Ask Him to give you a truly repentant heart. Make every effort to put things right again. Then the way will be clear and your prayers can rise up to God.

March 21
God, who is love, gives us a ray of light every day, no matter how dark that day may be: help, a solution, an encouragement, a token of His love. Look for this light. It is there. And you will see the way lit up before you.

March 22
Fearing the power of the atom, we look for a stronger power capable of protecting us from radioactive fall-out. If we knew this power, our problems would be solved. This power exists. It is the Lord, who made heaven and earth. Consequently, He has control over atomic power. Through His only-begotten Son, He says to those who believe in Him, 'Behold, I have given you authority ... over all the power of the enemy; and nothing shall hurt you.' – 'If they drink any deadly thing, it will not hurt them.' The Word of God holds true.

Luke 10:19; Mark 16:18

March 23
You are plagued by bitter thoughts and accusations against your fellow beings. You cannot understand why God allows them to do you so much harm. God, however, wants to help you. He warns you that your thoughts are going in the wrong direction and that you are unhappy, having linked yourself with Satan, the Accuser, who always makes us feel depressed.

Instead of accusing others, accuse yourself for the trouble you cause God every day with your sins and for the distress you have already caused many others. Thank the Lord for being gracious to you nonetheless, and then be kind to your neighbour. Thank God for His love in wanting to free you from your accusations against others by showing you your own faults. Now the moment has come when God wants to help you, cleanse you, free you from a critical attitude – and fill your heart with peace. Accept His help.

March 24

Do not keep your eyes on your problems and the impossibilities of your situation. Look beyond them. Remember, God is a Father. He is love. He has better things planned for you. God did not intend the difficulties to be the end of the story. He always has a solution to your problems, as well as joy and glory prepared for you.

March 25

A sign of a needy child is that he always goes to his father with his requests. A sign of a true father is the joy he feels when seeing the confidence his child has in him. This is what marks a true father-child relationship. God longs to have this relationship with us. Assume the status of a child, and you will experience an abundance of fatherly love, fatherly help and fatherly gifts. Be a genuine child towards God. Then the kingdom of heaven with all its treasures will be yours.

March 26

God is love. One of the characteristics of love is faithfulness. He will never leave you. He will never disappoint you. He will guide you and sustain you to the end. However, He is asking for your love in return. He entreats you, as it were, 'Trust Me when you are suffering and can no longer understand Me. Promise Me your loyalty as a token of your love.'

March 27

You complain that you do not receive much love. So many do not want to have anything to do with you. Some are even antagonistic towards you. This is not God's intention. He who is love wants to fill our lives with joy and blessings. This is why God wants to transform your plight. He shows you the way. Love, more than anything else, will overcome people who are against us or even hostile towards us. They will be won over by a sacrificial, selfless love, a love which does not repay evil with evil but rather blesses them and does them good. Go this way, which God in His love has shown you, and you will harvest love.

March 28

God the Father sees His children who have voluntarily chosen to go the way of the cross out of love for His Son. He cannot bear to see them suffer only, as they embrace poverty, lowliness and various sufferings for Jesus' sake. Time and again He refreshes His children and gives them joy. Live in expectation of this when you have a heavy cross to bear. Those who expect such refreshment and blessing receive it. However, those who resentfully close their hearts block God's grace and blessings.

March 29

You are at your wits' end. Look, there is Someone beside you, Someone who will advise you. When you feel helpless, He assures you of His presence and promises to come to your aid. It is your Lord and God, your heavenly Father. Trust in Him, the ever-present Father, whose help is always ready – and you will be helped.

March 30

As a true Father, God gives His children promises which He guarantees to fulfil. How can we doubt that God would keep His word, bringing His promises to pass? God will never fail us, for He is truth and He is love. Truly, He does not give us promises in order to disappoint us but in order to assure us of His help. Accept His promises. Cling to them and help will come.

March 31

The angels of God are not without feeling. We read in the Bible that they rejoice over every sinner who repents. How much more will God the Father rejoice! So it is possible for us to bring joy to the heart of the heavenly Father, though it may often seem otherwise. Usually we are only aware of grieving Him with our sin and wearying Him with our faults. How encouraging to know there is a way for everyone, including the worst sinner, to bring joy to the heart of the heavenly Father – contrition and repentance! *Luke 15:10; Isaiah 43:24*

April

April 1
Does the thought of war and catastrophe make you feel anxious? Your loving Father in heaven assures you, His small and fearful child, 'No evil shall befall you, no scourge come near your tent.' Yet you wonder how that could be if you were surrounded by utter devastation. The answer is that God would protect you through the mighty, strong angels He has ready for you. But then you ask, 'What if I die?' If this were to happen, angels would carry you home. The presence of Jesus and His love would enfold you so that no evil could overtake you. This, and nothing less, is what you would experience.

Psalm 91:10

April 2
You find it hard to accept God's will. What He has brought to pass seems to be ruining your life. But, whenever God shatters a life's dream, He will build up something new on the foundation of a broken and humble heart. He will give you something greater and far more wonderful, for God is love. He never takes from us anything which would have been best for us. He only seeks to deal with the impurities in our lives, so that He can build up much more wonderfully that which lies in pieces before us. He wants to fulfil the deepest longings of our hearts. Expect that, and you will be able to accept the will of God, finding all the comfort you seek.

April 3
When we are discouraged and there is no help in sight, let us say aloud, 'God is our refuge and strength, a very

present help in trouble.' God is able to help, because He is the Almighty. God wants to help, because He is love. Love always has to help, so help is guaranteed. The only time we will not experience help is when we condemn ourselves to remaining in misery by declaring there will be no help.   *Psalm 46:1*

April 4

You think you can no longer bear the burden that has been placed upon you. But the heavenly Father wants to comfort you, His child. Can you hear Him speaking in your heart? – 'Soon the dark valley will lie behind. Soon you will be greeted by bright beams of joy and bliss. You will laugh as much as you have wept.' Live in expectation of the moment your weeping turns to laughter. In heaven joy is for ever, but even here and now you may have a foretaste – perhaps tomorrow! Look forward to it.

April 5

God's heart is filled with love towards us. He encourages us to bring Him our requests in a childlike spirit. Being a Father, He rejoices whenever He can make us happy and pour out His goodness upon us. Now He is saying to you, as it were, 'Behave like a real child towards Me. Do not be shy but daily bring your requests, big and small, to Me your Father.' – Jesus has promised that the Father will give us good gifts when we ask Him. Try it out!

Matthew 7:11

April 6

God does wonders. It is part of His nature to do so, for He is the Almighty. He can create new life. He can do things that are impossible for human beings. However, today as long ago, our unbelief hinders Him from displaying His wonder-working power. This hurts God and is to our disadvantage. He is waiting for people who will turn to Him when they are in distress and sing His praises, declaring, 'Thou art the God who workest wonders.' By proclaiming God as the God who does wonders and by praising His power and greatness, you will experience His miracles in your life – but not otherwise.

Psalm 77:14

April 7

God is present everywhere. He is all-powerful. He rules the universe. He searches the depths. But it is in His care for the tiniest things that His greatness is most wonderfully demonstrated. Nothing escapes His notice. He has counted even the hairs on our heads. Whoever has eyes to see the greatness of God and His fatherly love in His attention to detail has truly fathomed God's nature and glory. Ask Him to give you such eyes. Then you will be able to see traces of God's greatness everywhere, and even in the smallest incidents you will have the assurance that He is guiding you.

April 8

You agonize about yourself. You are such a difficult person. You cannot accept how you are. But God, who has created you and who loves you, wants to help you. He shows you the way. Accept yourself for what you are; and, through Jesus, God will turn you into what you are to be, for God gives grace to the humble.

April 9

Learn a song which has power to banish all fears, doubts and worries. It is the song of love for the Father, and this is how it goes: 'My Father, my dearest Father!' Who sings it? – Christians who have really become children of the heavenly Father, living in dependence upon God. Trusting, small and humble, they are at home in the Father's house, where this song is constantly sung. Let it be your song and you, too, will find that it banishes cares and fears.

April 10
The Father never forgets those who suffer. They remind Him of His only-begotten Son in His sufferings. This is why the Father's heart is drawn to them in His infinite, compassionate love. Believe this.

April 11
Times of distress have shown that God is more mindful of His children than ever and sends them help. So let us trust Him, come what may, saying with the psalmist, 'Thou hast been my help, and in the shadow of thy wings I sing for joy.' This is what God expects of His children. Affirm again and again, 'I have a helper – my God and Lord. In times of trouble I will not only be hid under His wings, but I will also be able to sing for joy.' Such a declaration of faith will comfort and strengthen you.

Psalm 63:7

April 12
God loves the humble and insignificant, those who do not think much of themselves or seek prestige but are willing to be reproved and ignored. The Father draws near to them in His loving-kindness, bringing help and comfort. He bestows upon them His good gifts, for which they pray. So choose to walk in lowliness. Be humble in spirit and you will receive His gifts.

April 13

Those who let go of earthly securities in their lives, becoming entirely dependent upon God, will discover in times of hardship that they have done the right thing. God is the best insurance, His the only lasting security. His resources never fail. You can turn to Him at any time, in any situation, and He will take care of your needs. So let go of earthly securities.

April 14

If we want God to answer our prayers, we need to pray the kind of prayers He has promised to answer. Jesus tells us that one of these is the prayer in His name. Prayerfully mention to God the Father the name of Jesus, His beloved Son, who did everything for us. His name is a key which opens the Father's heart. Ask to be shown concerns in keeping with Jesus' mind and will; pray for these concerns in His name; then God will not be able to resist your request. The name of Jesus moves His heart to act on our behalf, for the Father cannot refuse any request of His Son. This is why Jesus says, 'The Father will give you whatever you ask of him in my name.' Ask like this. Then you will experience the fulfilment of your prayers.   *John 16:23 GNB*

April 15

A young child cannot do everything that grown-ups can. He is dependent upon the help of adults and naturally looks to them for help. And he thinks it just as natural that grown-ups send him here and there. He does what he is told. He accepts correction and discipline readily. Whoever is like a child in his relationship with God will experience what the Father in heaven has promised to the small and helpless: His loving care, His help, His miracles.

April 16

God, your Father in heaven, often leads you along difficult paths you do not like. The time has come for you to learn a lesson: Want only what He wants. Whoever has learnt this lesson, whoever can wholeheartedly accept the will of God in every situation, has learnt something which will fill his life with peace and joy. Even during the most difficult leadings he will be happy and at peace, for he is resting in the will that is always best. Start practising with the smaller issues in life and pray, 'Your will be done.' Then you will be able to rest in God's will in times of hardship and be victorious.

April 17

Because God is love and because He loves you, His heart longs to see evidence of your love. In spirit He shows you His only-begotten Son, who for love of us gave up all that was dear to Him. Now God is asking how you have thanked Him and what you have given up for His sake. Do not just give the Lord gifts that have been entrusted to you. Give Him your very self, your freedom, your wishes and desires, your whole heart and life. Such a sacrifice will bind you to God, uniting you with Him. Then you will have found the greatest treasure in heaven and on earth, and you will be a truly happy person.

April 18

God, the great and almighty Lord, does not perform His miracles like a magician. He performs them as your loving Father. Love can only reveal itself to hearts which are open – prayerful, trusting, expectant. Love is sensitive, so does not force its miracles upon us. Only those who have a trusting, childlike relationship with the Father will experience the miracles and great deeds of God.

April 19

You are downhearted. You cannot rejoice in God. Start thinking of what your heavenly Father means to you. He is a God who helps. He is your loving Father, who always has thoughts for your good. He will complete the work He began in your life, preparing you for heavenly glory. He is almighty and offers you shelter and protection. He has given His only-begotten Son for your redemption. As you think about these different truths concerning God and praise Him for them, sadness will yield and joy will be kindled anew in your heart.

April 20

As a child of the heavenly Father, you cannot be bold enough in putting your faith in His love and power. A bold faith evidently pleases God, otherwise He would not challenge us so often to be bold in faith. Indeed, God rejoices over such a faith. He cannot disappoint those who are bold in asking and in believing, provided they walk according to His commandments.

April 21

Those who feel helpless, weak and small will not be lost in the storms of affliction and turmoil of war. The Father's arms are strong enough to carry them. There is one thing He cannot do: He cannot let them fall into the abyss. So place yourself in the Father's arms, and you will be securely held and hid. He will carry you through every storm.

April 22

You are weeping bitterly. Have you considered the fact that you are not forgotten now? Someone is watching you with compassion: your heavenly Father. In His love

He has already thought of a way to help you. Your suffering touches His heart. He sees it. He already has comfort and help prepared for you. Believe this!

April 23

What is the way to happiness? – Total commitment to God. That means total surrender of your will to the will of God at every moment. This is the foundation of all happiness. Whoever has submitted his will to God's will, and renews this commitment again and again, is free from destructive self-will and oppressive worries. Rather, he rests peacefully in the will of God, in the loving will of the Father, who has the very best of intentions for His children. That makes for happiness.

April 24

God is holy and righteous. He is stirred to anger by sin and stretches out His hand in judgment over a sinful humanity, which has fallen away from Him. But to those who love Him and live according to His commandments, He offers His hand, ready to help and deliver. For them the scripture holds good: 'In the shadow of his hand he hid me.' Who will experience this in times of distress, war and divine judgment? – Those who claim this verse as a promise from the Lord. *Isaiah 49:2*

April 25

God is great, almighty and full of glory. Unlike us weak, helpless, limited human beings, God is perplexed by nothing. For Him, the word 'impossible' does not exist. Whenever we see no way out of a situation, no answer to a problem, He wants us to experience that 'with God all things are possible' – provided we believe that He is able. God expects our faith to be kindled by the 'impossible'.

That is why He leads us into such circumstances and situations.

When we believe the promises of God in our troubles and seemingly hopeless situations, we will discover how the impossible becomes possible. Blocked roads, as it were, will be cleared. People's hearts will be changed. The greater the hopelessness seems to be, the greater the Lord will prove to be. *Matthew 19:26*

April 26

God can never give up on a soul. He would first have to lose His own identity. But that cannot be, for He is eternal and His fatherly heart is nothing but love. In all your trials and temptations, in your struggles against sin, you can be sure of this: The fatherly heart of God will not give up on you. His heart pulsates for you in love. He wants to help you. He wants to set you right. And this He will accomplish.

April 27

You long for streams of blessing to flow from your life. God in His love wants to fulfil your wish. This is why He places an altar in every human life, an altar where He seeks sacrifices offered to Him in love. Only when there are sacrifices upon the altar, can the flame of sacrifice burn. To the extent that this flame blazes, God shines from your life. May your flame burn brightly, setting others on fire and blessing them.

April 28

Have you resigned yourself to the difficulties and sins in your life? Do you think that nothing will change? As long as this is your attitude, there will be no change in your situation. Not until you begin to reckon with God, who still performs miracles today and who always has help in store, will there be a difference. In faith praise His omnipotence over the impossibilities in your life. Prayerfully pronounce the promises of God and hold them up before Him as an IOU which has to be paid. Then you will experience the miracles of God, His help, a transformation in your life and in the hearts and situations of others.

April 29

You ask what is the quickest way out of your suffering. That should not be your primary concern. More important than anything else is that you suffer in the right way, so that your suffering will bear fruit; then you will not have suffered in vain. Take care that you suffer patiently and that you humble yourself under the mighty hand of God. When you ensure that you have the proper attitude towards your suffering, all false considerations will give way and you will experience an overwhelming victory in your suffering. Then your suffering will bear fruit for eternity.

April 30

You complain that everything around you is cold and lifeless. You are lonely in your family, in your circle of acquaintances, in your church. But that cannot be God's will. As your loving Father, He wants you to be loved and happy and He shows you the way: Give others much love, and you will harvest love.

Supposing that your heart were dead and cold and incapable of loving, even so there is a flame that could set it alight. It is the flame of love which burns in the Father's heart and which has flared up mightily in Jesus. Let God's heart enkindle you, and you will become a flame of love. Your love will be like a sun; it will shine upon all the cold hearts around you with goodness and kindness, setting them on fire with love. Then you will no longer be lonely.

May

May 1

You are right in thinking it will be darker than ever on earth if a war of extermination breaks out; in fact, it will be night everywhere. However, at the darkest point, the light of God will shine most brightly for those who belong to Him. Words written long ago will come true: 'Darkness shall cover the earth ... but the Lord will arise upon you, and his glory will be seen upon you.' In His light you will be able to walk step by step.   *Isaiah 60:2*

May 2

God's disciplinary measures and judgments demand a decision. Some people become hardened and embittered when judgment comes upon them; others experience a turning-point which brings healing and happiness. What would you like chastening to bring you? The choice is yours. Whoever humbles himself beneath the chastening hand of God will experience transformation, grace and blessing.

May 3

The eyes of God are searching the earth for those who believe. Through men and women of faith He can do great deeds; through them He can glorify Himself, demonstrating His power, His glory and His miracles before all the world. It must grieve the Father deeply to see the many servants Satan has to do his work. God the Father has so few children filled with zeal to glorify His name here on earth by trusting Him implicitly and, in obedience to His Word, launching out in faith. His eyes are watching to see whether you will commit yourself to walking in faith.

May 4

Why do we want independence from God? Why do we separate ourselves from Him? Often the unconscious motive is this: 'Then I no longer have to obey God's will.' However, if we are not interested in God's will and His commandments in our everyday life, God will not be interested in us in time of need. During the famine the prodigal son had to pay dearly for his alienation from his father: he did not receive any help. Nor will we, unless we repent and are prepared to live according to the will and commandments of God.   *Luke 15*

May 5

You long to come closer to God. You long for that deep intimacy with your heavenly Father. But you do not know how to attain this. Why not? You must be avoiding that which would bring you closer to God. It is through our cross that we draw nearer to God. Whoever embraces his cross lovingly will be united with Jesus and the Father. But whoever flees the cross, whoever protests against it in his heart, flees from God and is separated from Him.

May 6

Why does God draw near to the weak and the powerless? He is filled with compassion for them. Apart from Him, they have no helper; they must rely on the strength and greatness of their heavenly Father. And because they trust Him implicitly, He sends them help. Happy are the poor: they will taste the bounty of God's goodness.

May 7

You think that the darkest hour of your life has come. Then know that this is your hour of testing, the most crucial hour in your life. It is the hour in which God, your heavenly Father, is testing you to see whether you will trust Him in darkest night. All you have to say is: 'My Father, I do not understand You, but I trust in Your love.' Then great things will have been accomplished in you for time and for eternity.

May 8

The psalmist prayed, 'O Lord … hasten to my aid!' The Spirit of God prompted this prayer, because God really does hasten to our aid. Like every good father, He comes quickly when His child is in distress; indeed, He cannot come fast enough when you call to Him in your need. But do you really call upon Him? Prayerful trust in the Father is the solution to life's hardships, worries and difficulties. Therefore, do not brood over your troubles. Bring them to God. Cry out to Him, and the answer will not fail to come.   *Psalm 22:19*

May 9

In the Gospels Jesus proclaims holy, eternal laws of God. He says that people who follow His call to give up their rights and demands, their possessions and that which has become dear to them, will be wonderfully provided for: the heavenly Father Himself will take care of them. He wants them to have a share in His inheritance even here on earth. So commit yourself to letting go of that which is dear to you. Then in accordance with the eternal laws of God, you will be richly blessed.

May 10

As a Father, God wants to have His children very close to Him. He has opened wide the door to His house, paving the way through the suffering and death of His Son. Now the Father is waiting for us to draw closer to Him with each new day. Every new commitment, every loving act of trust, binds us more tightly to the Father.

May 11

Fear of what lies ahead is almost devouring your soul. Leave behind everything that makes you afraid. Go forward in spirit, and place yourself under the shadow of His wings. Begin to sing for joy, because you have a refuge which the Father has prepared for you. There you will be secure in times of trouble. You will be hidden in the hands of the Father, who lovingly cares for you.

May 12

What do you think the coming days and weeks will bring? Expect good things. God is good and, as a Father, He has good things in store for His child. However, to the wicked and distrustful, God seems a harsh master. Distrustful of God and His intentions, they erect in their hearts and lives a barrier against tokens of His goodness – and will harvest what they have sown. They will be unhappy and remain so, for we receive what we expect from God. So expect good things from Him.

May 13

The grandeur of God's creation with its gigantic mountains and vast oceans tells us how great God is. It also shows us how small we are. Yet we are still presumptuous enough to dare to pit our will against the will of God, the will of the almighty Creator and Lord, and to rebel against Him. We have lost the right perspective as regards our relationship with God. God's awesome creation has something to teach us. It is calling us to humble ourselves before the Almighty with our whole being, to worship Him and to commit our wills to Him. His will is best, because it is the will of a Father who is nothing but love.

May 14

Perhaps you have been sidelined through sickness or age. You seem to be up against a brick wall. You want to live and work; you hunger for joy – yet you already seem to be counted among the dead. But the living God, who raised Jesus from the dead, wants His children to be filled with life and joy. Seek this life in Him, not in health, a new occupation, or anything else. Then you will find lasting, unclouded happiness. This is why God in His love has brought you out of a life filled with human joys and pleasures. He wants to give you true life. Believe this.

May 15

God our Father allowed His only-begotten Son to suffer. Like a lamb led to the slaughter, Jesus did not return insult for insult, or utter threats, when He suffered. Now God is looking for the characteristics of the Lamb in His children. Always choose to follow Jesus' example, and you will have the spiritual authority you desire. God in His love wants to give it to you. It has been promised to those who are lamblike.   *1 Peter 2:23*

May 16

You are agonizing over God's dealings. You can no longer understand Him. But that is only natural. If we sinful, created beings could always understand God in His thoughts and leadings, He would no longer be God, whose ways and thoughts are higher than ours. We cannot comprehend them. Yet they are always wonderful, always inspired by love. He has our best interests at heart and will accomplish His eternal purposes wonderfully, bringing everything to a marvellous conclusion. Play your part now by accepting yourself for what you are: a mere creature who can never understand God but who can trust Him unreservedly. Then you will be free from mental anguish.

May 17
You do not know how God will solve your problems. God will not tell you in advance. You do not need to know beforehand how He will do it. But one thing is certain: As your Father, God will solve your problems. May this knowledge be enough for you. Praise His love which cannot do other than help you, and you will have peace of heart.

May 18
Making ourselves independent of God and breaking with Him is sin. It is an affront to the Father's love. It makes His heart ache. He appeals to us to turn around and not to make our decisions on a human level but in dependence upon Him. Your heavenly Father is waiting for this proof of your love. He is longing for you to live in complete dependence upon Him as His child. He wants you to have a loving relationship with Him. Do not keep Him waiting.

May 19

You are in suffering. All is dark. You do not know what to do. You feel helpless and cannot see a way out. Your loving Father in heaven sees that you are in distress and calls to you, as it were, 'If you are in darkness, I want to be your light. If you are in suffering, I want to be your comfort. If you are helpless, I want to be your helper. If you are perplexed, I want to be your counsellor.' Listen to His voice. Then your heart will become quiet.

May 20

You are longing to experience God's love. When will you experience it most? – When you love Him. This, more than anything else, causes Him to open His heart of love. How do you show that you love Him? – By wanting what He wants; by agreeing to His thoughts and complying with His plans for you; by placing your confidence in Him, even when you do not understand His actions and He gives you a cross to bear. His Son carried the cross of the world. Follow Him with your own cross, thus putting your love for God into action. In response He will let you taste His love for you.

May 21

From all eternity God in His love and tender care has thought of His children who would have to live in these dark times. In His Word He has prepared comfort for them, saying that all who call upon the name of the Lord will be delivered. Call upon His name now, then you will be comforted and, in the day of trouble, receive help.

Joel 2:32

May 22

Let us accept the tremendous status which our Lord Jesus Christ has obtained for us: to be sons of God, sons of our Father in heaven. Because of our sonship the Father bestows His inheritance upon us. Like the father in the parable of the prodigal son, He says, 'All that is Mine is yours.' Even here on earth He lets His children share in His power and His possessions. And one day, when they have grown to full maturity, reflecting the image of Jesus, they will inherit everything in the Father's kingdom.

Right now, however, you may be a pauper, sitting in rags. You are complaining about all the things you do not have and are feeling miserable. But it is your own fault that you are spiritually impoverished and have so many needs. You are not availing yourself of the inheritance which is yours. All your needs would be supplied and you would be richly blessed if you would only hold out your hands in faith.   *Luke 15:31*

May 23

Childlike trust has power. If an earthly father finds it irresistible, how much more so the heavenly Father, who is the perfect example of fatherhood and whose very nature is love! And love is won over most quickly by childlike trust. So practise trusting.

May 24

God the Father has a goal for our lives. He does not intend our lives to be barren. On the contrary, we are to produce abundant fruit. This is why the Father comes to us as the gardener. Wisely He cuts back the branches, so that they do not bear fruit in the first years. The more He prunes, the more fruit they will bear in years to come.

Jesus has given us this picture for those times when we seem to be bearing no fruit. Our lives seem to consist only of suffering. It is as if we were being reduced to nothing. In such times we should rejoice in the assurance that we are being prepared for great fruitfulness.

May 25

You see the beauty of creation. You see how wonderfully God created every flower, every animal. No two are identical. But people are a thousand times more valuable to God than all the glory of nature. He created them in His image, calling them His children. He delivered up His only-begotten Son to death for them. How very precious, therefore, are you to God! May this knowledge comfort you when doubts fill your heart. It is true – you are loved!

May 26

No human being has ever been so grieved and offended by sin as God. Yet no human being has ever uttered such words of infinite mercy to the offenders as God has done. Now we sinners are to be merciful to one another. God has a right to expect this in response to His compassion. Be merciful to your neighbour if he hurts you, so that God's mercy towards you will not turn to blazing wrath, as in the parable of the unforgiving servant.

Matthew 18:34

May 27

The Lord says, 'My compassion grows warm and tender. I will not execute my fierce anger.' This is what God the Father's heart is like. How can I gain access to this heart? It is closed to the self-righteous, to the high and mighty, to the proud, to those who feel intellectually superior.

But it is wide open to the humble, to the broken-hearted, to those who grieve over their sins. Upon them He pours out the abundance of His merciful love. The Father is calling you to go this way, so that He can reveal His heart to you and you can taste His loving-kindness.

Hosea 11:8-9

May 28
Do not be too concerned about the troubles ahead. Focus your thoughts on God your Father and on the help He already has for you. Turn your eyes upon God. Look, He is on His way! He comes when all is dark and hopeless. He comes to help.

May 29
God tore His beloved Son from His heart and delivered Him up to rebels and murderers. The sight of His Son's affliction made the Father's heart ache. Yet He bore this for us, because His love for us is so great. This being so, He should surely receive a continual harvest of thanksgiving from His children, thanksgiving expressed in trust even when we cannot understand Him.

May 30
God makes us an exceptional offer, saying in effect, 'Ask much, and it will be given you. Heaven and earth are Mine. All My messengers are at My disposal, ready to serve Me and to carry out My commands. They are sent forth to serve you – ten thousand times ten thousand – as a powerful force. What more do you need? Ask for much, ask Me for big things, and you will receive accordingly!'

Hebrews 1:14; Daniel 7:10

May 31

What if a major war breaks out, triggering off a world disaster? How would you cope with your fears? Trust God. Believe that when fear is about to overwhelm you, His peace and comfort will be greater than ever – yes, even greater than your fears. Firmly count on this, and be assured that you will experience what you believe.

June

June 1

Frequently it is we Christians who fall into the sin of living our lives independently of God. Basically, we do as we please. And often, like hypocrites, we try to cover up our sin of living our lives apart from the Father. We excuse ourselves.

Instead, we should examine ourselves to see how far we are actually living in childlike dependence upon the Father in the nitty-gritty of everyday life. Let us ask the Holy Spirit for light in this matter. Our lives will be fruitless if, in our self-will, we plan them independently of God. The more we depend upon God, even in the smallest things of life, the more fruit we will reap one day above, for we will have learnt to do everything in God.

June 2

Suffering creates glory. Yet so often we are unhappy in our suffering. Not a glimmer of God's love, comfort and glory penetrates our hearts. But our heavenly Father, who is love, knows what will comfort us. He urges us not to bear our cross like a slave who is forced to, but out of love for Jesus. When we bear it trusting in the Father's love and committed to His will, then our cross will begin to shine. We will become happy and we, too, will shine in His love. *2 Corinthians 4:17*

June 3

You are worried about how you will get through the desert stretches in your life – how you will cope with loneliness, illness, difficulties, hopeless situations ... But God is not worried that we go through such periods. His message to us could be summed up like this: 'If you are in the wilderness, I will prove Myself as your Father. Once long ago I provided the children of Israel with quails and manna when they were in the desert and had nothing to eat. I am the same today. I will go before you, too, by day in the pillar of cloud and by night in the pillar of fire. I will pave the way for you. With My presence I will bring you comfort and new strength. What more do you need?'

June 4

Suffering and God's disciplinary measures have left your heart sore. Like a child, place yourself in your Father's arms and let Him love you back to health. God never wounds His child without healing and refreshing him. Come, because He is waiting to do something good for you, His hurting child.

June 5

The heart of the Father is the source of all love. If a person refuses our plea for help, we appeal to his heart, to his sympathy, to his compassion. Who can express what God the Father's heart is like! Before His love all human love pales. No one calls upon the divine heart of the Father in vain. It overflows with compassion and mercy. Those who appeal to the heart of God in the assurance of His love have never been disappointed.

June 6

You would like to know the Father. Our Lord Jesus Christ wants to lead you to Him. But He can only bring you to the Father if you follow the way He went as the Father's only-begotten Son: the way of the cross. The path that Jesus trod was marked by poverty, lowliness, obedience and disgrace. To this day it is the path leading to the City of God, to the Father's house. Go this way, and you will come to know the Father and His love. He opens His heart to those who follow in Jesus' steps.

June 7

God the Father is seeking people who will listen to the lament of His heart: 'My people have committed two evils: they have forsaken me, the fountain of living waters, and hewed out cisterns for themselves, broken cisterns, that can hold no water.' – 'When they had fed to the full, they were filled … therefore they forgot me.' – 'O my people, what have I done to you? In what have I wearied you? Answer me!'

The Father's pain can only be relieved through the love of His children. We express our love for Him when we shed tears of repentance, when we trust Him, when we are willing to be true children of His – obedient, humble and dependent upon Him. God is waiting. Again and again He asks us to love Him. Who would want to hurt and disappoint His heart of love?

Jeremiah 2:13; Hosea 13:6; Micah 6:3

June 8

You are sad. Why? – Because you are living in yourself and not in God. Remember that God is present. You are not alone for a single moment. He surrounds you. He sees you. He bears everything with you. He wants to help you. Always live in the assurance that God is present. The awareness of His presence will transform everything for you, and your sadness will disappear.

June 9

God wants to live within us. In His love He longs to make His dwelling-place in our hearts. However, we must love Him. Otherwise He will not come. So let us keep on asking for love for God and our neighbour, and let us practise it. Love draws God to us. Could there be anything more wonderful than God making His dwelling-place in our hearts?

June 10

Maybe you do not find it hard to believe that God the Father will help you in your personal problems and carry you through. However, you are worried about what will happen when a time of great affliction descends upon us all. But you can be sure that His help will be proportionate to the disaster. Times of distress, terror and calamity have always been an opportunity for God to prove His glorious might. Consider this verse: 'It is thou who hast made the heavens and the earth by thy great power and by thy outstretched arm! Nothing is too hard for thee.'   *Jeremiah 32:17*

June 11

The eyes of God are looking for one thing: faith. God is looking for children who, in the night of distress and suffering, live in hope of the morning and sing of its dawning. Trust like this wins over the heart of the Father, and children like this will always experience the morning, the rising sun. Be such a child.

June 12

You wonder why you have to tread pathways fraught with suffering. Only paths through the night lead to the light. God, who loves you, wants all your ways to end in light, in great joy. This is why He is now leading you through the night.

June 13

What is the greatest gift God can grant us? – Himself, His nature, which is love. He does not want to keep this love for Himself. He wants to share it with us. This is why He sent Jesus, love manifest in the flesh. Jesus brought this love to earth in order to redeem us to love. Let us draw love from the fountain of grace, His heart. Then we will have the greatest gift, the greatest happiness for time and for eternity – love. Nothing can make us so happy as loving.

June 14

Are you seeking? For what are you seeking? Something satisfying, something that brings happiness? God's answer is: 'You will seek me and find me.' God, who made you, knows and loves you, wants to give you what you are seeking. Are you seeking to be loved? Are you seeking security? In Him alone will your deepest needs be met. Do you seek fulfilment? Do you seek someone who is completely available for you, someone to love and confide in? The One who does not lie, who cannot deceive, promises to give life abundantly. So turn to Him. He loves you. He will answer you and fulfil the longings of your heart. He cannot, and will not, disappoint you.

Jeremiah 29:13; John 10:10

June 15

You cannot understand how God, who calls Himself a Father, can give you such a heavy cross to bear. Have you perhaps forgotten that we are all sinners? Sinners need a cross and suffering in their lives in order to be disciplined, purified and transformed. Otherwise they would never reach the goal of God's glory. Without holiness no one will see the Lord. *Hebrews 12:10, 14*

June 16

Look at the fatherly hands of God. Look at the way they work in the lives of human beings. These fatherly hands place the robe of righteousness and the most precious ring of divine love on those who approach the Father like the prodigal son and who say in deep contrition, 'Father, I have sinned against heaven and against You.' When your sins and failures make you sad, place yourself in these fatherly hands. They will soothe your pain and show you infinite kindness.

June 17

Those who love us are glad when they see us joyful. They do everything they can to make us happy. But no one loves us as much as God. Nothing brings more joy to His heart than seeing His children happy. Let us believe this of Him and, in believing, let us be happy like little children. When we expect good things from our Father, we bring Him joy. Let us not grieve His loving heart by doubting Him.

June 18

God loves us. This is why He trains and disciplines us like a true father bringing up his children. He stops showering us with His gifts when we use them selfishly or disobediently. But Jesus wants us to experience the kingdom of heaven with all its blessings, and so He keeps calling to us, 'Repent.' The heart of the Father is wide open to all who are sorry for their sins and turn from them. When we come in repentance, He can shower us with His goodness.

June 19

Say to God your Father, 'Thank You that I do not have to reckon only with money, natural ability and human resources. Your mighty hand that created the universe sustains me. You command, and the need is supplied.' – Help comes with faith and thanksgiving. It is ours for the asking.

June 20

Your heart is filled with anxiety. All peace has left you. You are gripped with fear of the apocalyptic time of destruction ahead. God your Father wants to help you; He wants to fill your heart with peace. Hear His cry, 'O that you had hearkened to my commandments! Then your peace would have been like a river.' In other words, accept the commandments of God as binding and do His will day by day. Then you will be one with God; this, in turn, will make you strong and fill your heart with peace. In times of great distress this peace will not leave you. It will be as an ever-flowing river, for its source is union with the will of God.   *Isaiah 48:18*

June 21

Whenever we feel helpless and inadequate, the moment has arrived for us to appeal to the Father in prayer and call down His love. At such moments His love will come to us as never before – if only we would believe this! These are the moments when we move the Father to have mercy upon us, to demonstrate His miraculous power, His help and kindness, and to pour out His love upon us. Let us take advantage of these moments. They are opportunities to experience the love and aid of the Father more than ever.

June 22

Perhaps you are complaining that God, who is love, has given you a cross that is especially heavy. Your heavenly Father would assure you, 'Your cross is not heavier than you can bear. If your cross is heavy, so too is the blessing hidden within it. Recognize My love in sending you a heavy cross. I reserve it for those dearest to Me, because I intend to give them special blessings. Discover the treasure in your cross by trusting that I have hidden a blessing within it.'

June 23

Can we ever measure the fatherly goodness of God? He always has the best interests of His children at heart, longing to bless and help them. He is intent upon making them happy. As His children we should respond by singing Him songs of praise. By proclaiming how good the heavenly Father is and by thanking Him, we open His hands; and blessings, grace and tokens of His fatherly goodness will stream down upon us. Give thanks more often and you will receive more; yes, you will receive abundantly.

June 24

God has a heart full of love. That is why He consoles us like little children, as if saying, 'Nowhere are you beyond My reach. Even if you have gone to the ends of the earth and are perhaps in peril of your life – I am there also. I am with you to help you, to protect you and to sustain you.' So answer Him, 'Yes, Lord, You are everything to me. And whoever has You has all he needs, even in death.'

June 25

Before the beginning of time God planned in His heart how He would lead you. There could be no better way, and it will bring you to a glorious goal. The Father is waiting for you, His child, to accept this leading as coming from Him and to follow it wholeheartedly. Say to Him, 'Thank You, Father, for leading me the best way.' As you give thanks, your eyes will be opened to see the blessings of God upon your way.

June 26

You have lost courage. You are on the verge of despair. Your sin seems to be binding you with chains, making you feel like a prisoner. But God your Father loves you. He does not leave His children to their fate. On the contrary, He has provided a door out of the dark prison. This door is repentance. The penitent sinner receives forgiveness through the blood of Jesus. And forgiveness makes everything new – you, your whole life. Such creative power lies in repentance that it even works retrospectively, redeeming the past and restoring what has been destroyed by sin.

June 27

We may claim it is too hard to believe in the love of God, but God has proved that He loves us. Out of love for us He suffered immeasurably, delivering up His Son into the hands of sinners. He suffered with His Son when He was tormented and mistreated beyond recognition and then finally killed. So whatever God does is always love, even when we do not understand His actions. It is at these times that we should love Him most – for the sake of His great act of love, the sacrifice of Jesus Christ. We should honour Him with our trust.

June 28

God is a Father of love. It is the nature of love to care for others. So let your Father take care of everything that concerns you and is oppressing you. Scripture says, 'Do not worry about tomorrow; it will have enough worries of its own.' As a child, you are not capable of making arrangements for your future anyway. Leave the overall planning to your Father. He is all-wise, all-powerful, all-knowing. He only expects you to take care of those things assigned to you day by day. Leave further developments to God. 'Wonderful in counsel, and excellent in wisdom', He will bring everything to a glorious conclusion.   *Matthew 6:34 GNB; Isaiah 28:29*

June 29

You would like to show God your love, but you do not know how. Give Him your will. This means giving Him everything. From now on choose what He desires. Choose His way, the way in which He wants to lead you. Choose to have that which He gives you; equally, choose to do without that which He withholds from you or which He takes from you. Surrender to Him all your personal wishes and desires. Then you will have shown that you love God above all else. God will respond by coming to you and making His home with you.   *John 14:23*

June 30

When a child is fearful, his mother takes him in her arms and keeps him from seeing whatever is making him afraid. The Father in heaven will do the same for us. In times of trouble He will shelter us, covering our eyes and taking us in His arms so that we hardly see anything of the horrors. Enfolded in love, we will have only a sense of security. His presence will be a protective wall around us. He will carry us through.   *Psalm 27:5*

July

July 1

Perhaps you are saying, 'I have received so few of God's good gifts. He has fulfilled so few of my wishes.' Why is your life so poor? You certainly cannot blame God. Let God ask you a few questions: 'Have you fulfilled My wishes and My will by living according to My commandments? Have you given Me first place in your life and loved Me above all else? Have you loved your fellow beings with a love that bears all things, endures all things and does not become resentful? Have you honoured your parents? Have you slandered anyone, lied, stolen or committed adultery?'

If you are wondering about unanswered prayer, there is a scripture telling who will receive from God the good things for which he has asked: 'We have confidence before God; and we receive from him whatever we ask, because we keep his commandments and do what pleases him.' So act according to the will of God, and you will experience the truth of His promise: 'I will rejoice in doing them good.'   *1 John 3:21-22; Jeremiah 32:41*

July 2

We often know about God but no longer have a vital relationship with Him. God stands outside our daily life, no longer relevant to us. If this is a picture of your spiritual life, it is high time you turned over a new leaf; otherwise you could find yourself in the same situation as the rich farmer in Jesus' parable. He worked and also made provision for his future without reference to God. Perhaps God will say to you as well, 'This night your soul is required of you.' How will you be able to stand before God if you are not rich in your relationship with Him? *Luke 12:20*

July 3

God the Father has shown us His greatest love by freely delivering up His only-begotten Son to torment and death on the cross for our sakes. And Jesus has shown us His greatest love by freely taking up His cross for love of us. Now God is waiting for us to take up our cross of our own free will and to bear it out of love for Him. With such an attitude we reflect the nobility of Jesus and will inherit great glory.

July 4

In Scripture you have the promise of God's fatherly love. When worries loom up like mountains before you, say to yourself again and again, 'The Father cares. He cares.' God will take care of everything as only perfect love can do, planning every detail with divine power and wisdom. Let this knowledge be turned into praise. When you thank Him for caring for you, your heart will be filled with comfort and peace.

July 5

When a little boy has a big, strong man at his side to stand up for him, he has all the help he needs. Often we feel weak, helpless and inadequate in the face of our troubles, difficulties and responsibilities. However, the Lord who has made heaven and earth assures us that He wants to stand up for us. When He challenges us to be of good courage, these are not empty words. What can we possibly lack when the Lord of lords assures us, 'I am with you ... I will help you'? *Isaiah 41:10*

July 6

Because God loves us as a Father, He is obliged to train and discipline us as His children. But it hurts Him. Being the very essence of love, He finds it hard to punish us. Believe in His love. Over and over again He is moved with pity for His child. He has to comfort him, encourage him, show him kindness and make him happy. Even His wrath is tempered with mercy. He says to us, as to His people long ago, 'Is Ephraim my dear son? Is he my darling child? For as often as I speak against him, I do remember him still. Therefore my heart yearns for him; I will surely have mercy on him.' Cling to this assurance.

Jeremiah 31:20

July 7

In spite of having come to a living faith in Jesus, some believers lapse into legalism, because they resist being moulded into true children, whose mark is trusting love. A true child of God will follow Jesus Christ as a disciple of the cross. He is prepared to lose his life, relinquishing all that is dear to him. Yet he also rejoices over the Father's good gifts. He delights in the beauty of nature and all that the Father has made. He takes pleasure in people and things given by God as a token of His fatherly love. He can love them without becoming over-attached or overdependent.

To live as true children of the Father, free from legalism but bound by love to Jesus' pathway, makes for happiness – and also inspires many who are far away to draw close to their heavenly Father.

July 8

God needs people who are persistent in prayer like the Canaanite woman who refused to be put off. He is waiting for people who, even on first receiving a stone instead of bread, nevertheless persevere and take God at His word. Jesus once asked, 'What man of you, if his son asks him for bread, will give him a stone?' No true father would! So say to your heavenly Father, 'You will never give me a stone when I ask for something!' In response to such a humble prayer God will turn the stone – even were it already in your hands – into bread. He stands by His word.   *Matthew 15:21-28; 7:9*

July 9

The door to the heavenly Father's house has been opened through Jesus Christ. Yet so often we live outside. Sadly, we have discovered so little about what it means to live in the Father's house. There a child is at home. Surrounded by joy and security, he knows he is loved and can come to the Father with all that is on his heart. He receives more advice and help than he could ever ask for or imagine. He is committed to the will of the Father and to all His leadings. In receiving the Father's forgiveness, he finds that his deepest needs are met. Jesus wants to draw us into the Father's house when He tells us that we should become like little children – dependent and without influence or prestige. Who will respond to His call?

July 10

God is a Father. He comforts us in view of impending hardships, assuring us that He knows those who trust in Him, promising that their trust will not be disappointed. Indeed, we have no reason to doubt such a God who with His Son Jesus Christ endured the depths of suffering for our sakes. At Calvary God proved the greatness of His love. And because God is eternally the same, He will also prove His love in times of great distress. Yes, He will take care of us and help us.

July 11

For what do you pray? Never forget to ask for repentance, for this is a prayer especially pleasing to the Father, one which He will not fail to answer. Repentance is a joyful experience because it drives us into the arms of God, to His very heart. When repentance has found room in your heart, a stream of joy will flow forth. Out of repentance comes new divine life, marked by love – and love creates happiness. The heavenly Father wants to give you this gift of repentance. He cannot bear to see anyone unhappy.

July 12

You believe in Jesus and this makes you a child of God the Father. Yet you say that you are not happy. The reason is that you are looking for happiness in the wrong place. Joy lies hidden in the cross. If you want to taste this joy, adopt a new attitude towards your cross. Accept it as a greeting from the Father, as a means of blessing. Expect your cross to bring you the happiness you desire. You will then experience the truth: Out of tears comes laughter; out of the cross comes joy.

July 13

'The Father himself loves you.' So says Jesus, who is the truth and who knows the Father's heart intimately. You really are loved by God the Father. Tell yourself over and over again, 'I am loved!' Trust in the Father's love will heal everything in your soul that needs healing.

John 16:27

July 14

As our Father, God has the right to delight in His children. He longs to find in them traces of His divine nature and rejoices when this is so. By submitting willingly to His discipline, believing in the redemption of Jesus, we will bring Him this joy, because we are being transformed into the image of His Son. Let us not keep the Father waiting so long to see His reflection in us. Rather, let us make every effort to present Him with Christlikeness – to His joy. Let us strive for holiness.

Hebrews 12:14

July 15

In the hectic rush of everyday life, little is accomplished that brings blessing. All great things of eternal value are born of times apart with God. So seek to have more quiet time alone with God. Nothing can replace abiding in His presence. The greater the stress at work and the more numerous the difficulties, the more time you should be spending alone with God. Prayer will give you the strength to stand firm during trials and temptations. Only your quiet times with God will enable you to cope with the pressures of life. Seek the presence of God. In His presence everything will be solved that you cannot solve yourself.

July 16

In order to attain important goals in our lives we are prepared at times to take risks. Now God, as our Father, is asking us to dare something else. He is waiting for people who, in obedience to His word, are willing to step boldly into the unknown, because they trust in His promise that all things are possible with Him. Such people will experience the wonderful deeds and miracles of

God today. They will say with the psalmist, 'By my God I can leap over a wall.'   *Psalm 18:29*

July 17

Even on the darkest day do not forget to say, 'Thank You, Father!' Especially on such days you will find it a great help to list the blessings the Lord has given you for body and soul. Giving thanks will make an overcast day bright. God sends dark days only to test you, to see whether you will remain faithful in giving Him the thanks you owe Him. Those who cannot give thanks on sad days have not yet learnt their lesson. Giving thanks when it does not come easily is a sacrifice. But only a thank *offering* – an act of thanksgiving which costs us something – is precious in God's sight and of real worth. God says, 'He who brings thanksgiving as his sacrifice honours me.'   *Psalm 50:23*

July 18

God yearns for people who behave like children towards Him and are dependent upon Him. As a Father, God would like to act on behalf of His children and care for them. However, if in our self-will we forcibly try to bring about a solution to our everyday problems, we will not experience His care and intervention. We will deprive ourselves of a most precious experience: the Father's loving care, resulting in a carefree, happy heart. So let go of your self-will and stop trying to cope with your problems yourself. Then God will help you.

July 19

Perhaps you are at your wits' end. You do not know how you are going to manage any longer with respect to your health, strength and work. But be assured, it is good when you reach the end of your resources. Then Someone else can step in and help you start afresh. A particularly relevant Bible verse is, 'Behold, I make all things new.' You will see this promise come true as you apply it to yourself.

God the Lord, who loves you, says in effect, 'I make all things new, and this holds good for you as well. But first you must bring Me your old life with all its sin. A new house can be built only when the old, dilapidated house has been torn down. Through the blood of Jesus I will blot out your sins and forgive you.' So come with your sins. Confess them to the Lord in the presence of a spiritual counsellor. Then you will be glad that you were at the end of your resources. It signified a turning-point in your life – the beginning of something new.

Revelation 21:5; Isaiah 43:18-19

July 20

God the Father is greater than all. What a wonderful assurance! His love is greater than all human love and all human willingness to help. The help which He can offer is greater than your difficulties. His forgiveness is greater than your burden of sin. And because God the Father is greater than all, He is also greater than any calamities that may yet come. In every hardship say, 'Father, You are greater than all.' Then you will experience the reality of these words. *John 10:29*

July 21

Our loving Father in heaven is deeply grieved when His warnings and disciplinary measures have no effect upon us. They miss the mark when we protest against His refining process, lashing out against His chastening hand. Words cannot tell what sorrow we cause the

Father when we respond in this manner. In reality we are destroying the work He wants to accomplish in us. So it is we who are to blame when He cannot transform us into the image of Jesus, as He wants to do through chastening; it is we who are to blame when He has to devise new ways of disciplining us for our good. Whoever humbly submits to God will be spared many disciplinary measures, much pain.

July 22

Since God is a father in the truest sense of the word, what could make Him more happy than a person who has a childlike relationship with Him, who comes to Him in complete trust and who expects gifts of love from Him? From millions of people the Father receives only mistrust, and that wounds His heart. Would you like to be someone who brings joy to God's heart? Then trust in His love. Trust Him completely.

July 23

Your cross is weighing heavily upon you. You can no longer believe in the love of God. Yet you say that you believe in Jesus Christ. If you believe in Him, you must also believe in God the Father, who is love. This means that everything the heavenly Father does is inspired by love, even when He chastens you by giving you a cross to bear. Precisely then is He refining you, making you ready to enter the heavenly glory. Your cross, which is now weighing heavily upon you, will transform you and lift you up to heaven. Love your cross. God has given you it as a key that will one day open the door to heaven. Do not lose this key. It is precious.

July 24

You are happy that God in His goodness has given you so much here on earth that is dear to you and enriches your life. Perhaps it is close friends or family; perhaps it is your career, your talents, your possessions, house and garden. Have you ever considered that you have much to give, since God in His love has given you so much? Give to Him who is worthy of all our gifts. Do not keep Him waiting for your presents. He is waiting for you to love Him in return.

July 25

Fear of the coming times of distress is almost strangling you. You think you can never be happy again. But then the voice of Someone reaches you – Someone who has known God from the beginning of time as His only-begotten Son. It is the voice of Jesus: 'Have faith in God.' – 'Will not God vindicate his elect, who cry to him day and night? ... I tell you, he will vindicate them speedily.'   *Mark 11:22; Luke 18:7-8*

July 26

We often think we are alone and forgotten. But we are mistaken. The eyes of God the Father are constantly upon us. He can see into our hearts. He perceives every emotion and thought, every sorrow and doubt. He looks upon us in infinitely merciful love. He is waiting for us to catch His glance and to let Him comfort and help us and set us straight with His love. He wants to guide us with His eyes. So look to Him.

July 27

God our Father is longing for us to be completely dependent upon Him. Why? – Because He who loves us yearns for us to return His love. Becoming dependent upon Him of our own free will is a sign that we love Him. It is a sign of trust. God shows His love to those who are prepared to be dependent upon Him. They will experience the bounty of His love.

July 28

God is the Almighty and He is also our loving Father. He intends our lives to abound in His wonders and blessings to the glory of His name. This will happen to the extent that we dare launch out in faith at His word. According to the measure of our faith will we experience God's miracles and glorify Him.

July 29

Do you feel weak and incompetent? If so, rejoice in the assurance of the Lord that His grace is sufficient for you. In His grace is everything you need. The strength of God, His grace and help are displayed most effectively in the weak. So you are actually rich when you are poor in the way of abilities and talents – that is, if you boast with the apostle Paul of your weakness, trusting in God's grace. *2 Corinthians 12:9*

July 30

You have lost all hope of help in your difficult situation and in view of the impending calamities which will bring terror to the whole earth. Put your trust in God. We have His promise: 'Call upon me in the day of trouble; I will deliver you.' Cling to this verse. Do not yield to despair, for, as the Bible warns us, 'If you will not believe, surely you shall not be established.' Those who trust and revere

God, expecting the best from Him, will experience grace and comfort. So it was long ago; so it is today.

Psalm 50:15; Isaiah 7:9

July 31
Who are the people who most experience God's loving care? – Those who take up their cross and follow Jesus patiently, humbly, looking to God alone for help. God sees the reflection of His suffering Son in them. That stirs His heart deeply and moves Him to show them kindness, to comfort and uplift them.

August

August 1

You think you are abandoned to the misery you have brought upon yourself by your sinning. If that were so, God would no longer be alive – God, who out of love gave His Son as an atoning sacrifice for sin, so that we might be saved. He provides a way out of all such distress: repentance. Repentance can even turn our sin into gain. God in His goodness gives penitent sinners many additional gifts: thanksgiving for His forgiveness; love for our Saviour Jesus; humility; hatred of sin; faith in the blood of Jesus, which cleanses from all unrighteousness. Who can comprehend God's merciful love towards sinners? So let us walk in the way of repentance.

August 2

It has grown dark upon the earth, and darkness is creeping into your heart. Be assured, God comes to look after His child whenever he is surrounded by darkness and afraid. He says, 'Fear not, I will help you.' The sun may no longer be shining upon you, but now the Lord wants to be your everlasting light, your joy and comfort. His light shines more brightly than the sun, and His joy is greater than your greatest sorrow. This holds good for even the darkest times. *Isaiah 41:13; 60:19-20*

August 3

Does it seem incompatible that a God of love, who counts our tears, can send us suffering and crosses, which cost us tears? The Lord's reply to that is, 'Blessed are you that weep now, for you shall laugh.' The blessing is hidden in love for the cross. Do you lack this love for your cross? Then you cannot be happy. Love your cross as a gift from your heavenly Father – and love will make it bearable. The secret of the love of the Father and the love of Jesus will be revealed to you and make you happy even amid tears.   *Psalm 56:8; Luke 6:21*

August 4

Who will experience in abundance the love and care, yes, the miracles of God the Father? – Those who have the courage to become poor in one area or another and trust God alone to provide for all their needs. God can demonstrate the greatness of His bounty and loving care in the lives of the poor. Should that not make us want to follow His call to lose our lives, letting go of that which is dear to us?

August 5

A child's prayer to God the Father is powerful and has the promise of being answered, for God loves children. He listens to the cries of little ones and helps them. However, born-again children of God are often in danger of losing their child status, which Jesus Christ won for them. It must be demonstrated in everyday life. It needs to be constantly strengthened by childlike dependence upon the Father, by willingness to be humbled, by dedication to the Father's will. The deeper our commitment, the more power our prayers will have.

August 6

You have to go through a desert period in your life. Your soul is in spiritual drought and darkness. But God is love. With Him there are no deserts without oases. You can be sure they are waiting for you. In joyful expectation go forward to find them.

August 7

We should not let a single day pass without asking God, 'Teach me to trust in Your fatherly love.' There is nothing we need more than such trust. Those who can trust the Father like a child will receive help in all their troubles. The gift of trust is a most precious gift, which the Father is waiting to give to those who ask.

August 8

You see where humanity is heading. The threat of a nuclear war and large-scale destruction hangs over the world because of humanity's sins. But your loving Father in heaven tells you in His Word that He is 'a shield to those who walk in integrity ... preserving the way of his saints'. He will make a path in the mighty waters for His saints, His chosen ones. He will lead them safely through fire, for they are precious in His sight and are in His care. For your part, make sure that you really belong to Him.

Proverbs 2:7-8; Isaiah 43:2

August 9

God answers prayer. His Word tells us so. But perhaps you ask: Does He really? Yes, He does, though often differently than we expect. God is a Father, and He will not give His child anything that would be harmful in body, soul or spirit. He alone in His infinite wisdom knows what is best for His child and gives him what he truly needs. In the long run you will see that God did answer your prayer: He has given you what you ultimately desired, even though He did not fulfil your specific request. If the Father has to withhold something from you for your own good, you can be sure that in another way His loving heart will give you even more than you asked. Open your eyes and see this truth. *1 John 5:14*

August 10

You keep thinking, 'Why does God, who says that He is a Father of love, lay this cross upon me?' Do not keep your eyes on yourself but on Jesus, who entered glory through the cross. Your cross is meant to be a ship carrying you to the City of God, where you want to go. To this day there is no other way to glory. It is the cross and suffering that prepare eternal blessedness for us, according to Scripture. So look forward with joy to the heavenly glory. In faith live even now as though already having attained the heavenly goal. Then the things that are difficult to bear will become easy.

Acts 14:22; 2 Timothy 2:12

August 11

Do not let happiness pass you by. You are being offered a life of joy and happiness, love and spiritual authority. This offer comes with a guarantee against disappointment – because the One making it is the Lord your God, who keeps His promises. In no time at all you could be happy and fulfilled. Just reach out.

When you open your hand, though, you first have to release your grip on whatever you are holding on to, possibly things incapable of ensuring happiness anyway, perhaps things which are not even good. Let go and place them beneath the cross of Jesus. God the Father has erected this cross out of love – the cross on which His Son hung so that we might find salvation and happiness. Only there can you find healing for your soul. Come to the cross daily with your sins and burdens. At Calvary they will be taken from you, and God will bless you and make you happy. Come to Jesus. He will fulfil the deepest longings of your heart.

August 12

Whoever lives like a happy and carefree child, completely dependent upon God, will experience God, as a Father, leading him in wonderful ways. He will see how God solves all his difficulties and problems, cares for him and intervenes on his behalf in every situation. It is wise to leave behind all human security and to seek only the Kingdom of God, His righteousness, His approval. Those who do so will find that all their needs are met.

August 13

Perhaps you are carrying a heavy burden. It seems to be mountainous, and you feel nearly crushed beneath the weight. You cannot imagine this mountain ever being moved. But God in His love has already planned a solution. Dig underground tunnels. Burrow your way through bit by bit. Finally the mountain will be undermined – and collapse. Then, where once there was a mountain, will be seen a new and marvellous work of God. And what are these underground tunnels? – Small steps of faith leading to victory.

August 14

God has powerfully demonstrated His love for us by revealing Himself, speaking to us and making known His will. He tells us what we should do and what is good for us. Nothing so grieves His heart as when we ignore His words and commands. If we love God, we will take His commandments seriously. Seeking to apply them, we find that doing the will of God brings happiness and blessing, for the will of God comes from a heart which has only good intentions concerning us, a heart which is nothing but love.

August 15
God as the Father of love will not let the sky above us grow dark without placing lights of promise in it. Look up and see them. They will lighten even your darkness.

August 16
Do not look down on the ordinary days that do not seem to contain anything special. Do not despise small opportunities or little strength. God loves the small and lowly – a little town like Bethlehem, a small nation like Israel. He encourages you by saying, 'A little one shall become a thousand, and a small one a strong nation.' That is a law in the Kingdom of God. Those who humbly live out the seemingly less important days, those who are faithful in the little things, will find that the Lord will place them in charge of much. They will experience and accomplish great things. *Isaiah 60:22 AV*

August 17
You feel spiritually dead. Perhaps for a long time you have been asking God for new spiritual life – but to no avail. Be assured that God, being love, likes to give – especially this new spiritual life. He is only waiting for you to take the path leading to this new life: the path of sacrifice. In sacrificing, we find life. To the extent that we make sacrifices will we be alive. So begin to give God something. Give Him of your time and money. Give Him things and people you cling to. Then you will come alive and be filled with the joy that God wants to give you.

August 18
You say, 'What I hoped for and tried to achieve has not worked out. The die is cast.' But even if it seems too late, it is not. You can still change the course of things. Call to

God in your distress. In His love He will advise you and show you how your failure can be turned into victory: by calling upon the victorious name of Jesus. Proclaiming His name over your failure will have a retrospective effect. In the victory of Jesus lies the dynamic for change.

August 19

God is love. Whoever loves has to be with the beloved, especially when the beloved is in distress, as we know from the Bible: 'I will be with him in trouble.' The Lord is present when the need is greatest – when, for example, wars flare up. He will surround us on all sides, protecting us from the advancing terrors. This the Almighty can do.

Psalm 91:15; 125:2

August 20

If a child is hurt or upset, he expects his father to take him in his arms and comfort him. How much more should we count on the love of our heavenly Father in such situations. His love is a thousand times greater than the love of all human fathers. Jesus' words, 'Come to me, all who labour and are heavy laden, and I will give you rest,' give us a glimpse of the Father's love. Let us come and experience the wonderful rest He gives.

Matthew 11:28

August 21

Whenever fear and anguish are about to overwhelm us, Jesus appeals, 'Believe in God, believe also in me.' What He is saying is this: 'Believe in the power of God, whose presence can transform hell into heaven. Then, when you are in distress, you will have a foretaste of heaven.' Stephen, the first Christian martyr, experienced this, as

have many others after him. Ours will be the same experience if we believe in the love of God. *John 14:1*

August 22

You think the way God is leading you is more than you
can bear. That cannot be. God is your Father. He does
not give His child more burdens than he can carry. If the
going is especially hard, you may be sure that His love
has also planned special blessings and help. So persevere
to the end. Great and wonderful things await you. Do
not focus on the way but on your destination. The way is
short and does not last long. But at the heavenly goal,
where all is joy and glory, you will remain for ever.

August 23

You say, 'I have no talents, no abilities, no energy. I am
good at nothing.' The Lord would answer, 'Then now is
the time for Me to act. I do not share My power with
human power. However, I do prove My power in those
who cannot achieve anything by themselves. In them My
power can become visible.' Rejoice in your inability and
weakness, for then the power of God will be demonstrated in your life, making you effective.

August 24

No love has been so ill-rewarded and bitterly disappointed as the love of the heavenly Father. No father has
ever loved so much and taken such great pains to bring
up and discipline his children as the Father in heaven; no
father has met with such rebellion and defiance in
return. Consequently, no heart deserves so much love
and joy as God's fatherly heart. To bring Him this is
worth living for.

August 25

God seldom gives His children a long-range view of the path they are following. He lets them see only the next stretch they have to cover. Why? – Because this is the best training in faith for the future, which still lies in darkness. Since God loves us, He wants to grant us the crown of faith one day. That is why He has to give us opportunities now to practise faith.

August 26

It hurts God the Father when we shut Him out of our lives. Sadly, although we call ourselves His children, we often do so. We want to get everything done by our own strength, resources and natural abilities. We think we have to take care of ourselves. But in so doing, we lose the most important thing of all – that vital relationship with our heavenly Father and His heart. Consequently, we miss out on those daily proofs of His love and the help which, in many situations of need, He alone can provide.

August 27

It depresses you to think about coming events. Look to the hills from where your help comes, for help will come. It will come from the God who made heaven and earth and who is the help of His chosen ones. Look away from all the perils here on earth; look to Him who has power to help in every situation. Your heart will then be transformed. You will become strong and confident. Fear and despair will yield.   *Psalm 121:1-2*

August 28

God is denying you the fulfilment of your fondest dreams. You are in great anguish. But there is a means of help. Say, 'My Father, what You deny me, I do not want to have. I only want what You have chosen for me.' There is power in such dedication of the will. It will cause your agonizing desires to yield, for a heart resting in the will of God is filled with peace and comfort.

August 29
You think that, when disaster strikes, you will be completely at the mercy of the forces of destruction. But God's Word tells us differently. It says, 'When the righteous cry for help, the Lord hears, and delivers them out of all their troubles ... Many are the afflictions of the righteous; but the Lord delivers him out of them all. He keeps all his bones; not one of them is broken.' So take care that you belong to the 'righteous' who, having been made right with God through the blood of Jesus, live according to the commandments of God. Then God's promise of special help and protection is yours.

Psalm 34:17-20

August 30
When following dark paths that seem to lead nowhere, be assured that the love of God always has a gracious outcome prepared for you. After dark days of suffering, the sun will smile upon you again. Live in this assurance, and even now your darkness will be turned to light.

August 31
In every situation think of these words: 'It is the Lord!' Then you will no longer become upset about circumstances or the way others treat you. Instead, you will see God at work in everything. Humble yourself beneath the hand of God in the knowledge that His loving heart intends only the best for you and will bring good out of

the harm caused by circumstances or people. Believe this. Then you will be spared much distress and turmoil, and you will gain the victory over inner conflict.

September

September 1
Whoever wishes to ask much of the heavenly Father, and to receive much, should obey His will and His commandments as a true child of His. Jesus says, for instance, 'Judge not, that you be not judged.' If we persist in being judgmental and speaking ill of others and do not repent, we will come under judgment ourselves. Sometimes God judges us by not opening His hand and answering our prayers. *Matthew 7:1*

September 2
In order to strengthen our faith, God has revealed to us who He is – love. Whenever you suffer greatly or cannot understand God's leadings, say again and again, 'God is love. God is love.' As you testify to this before the visible and invisible world, your confidence in God will become unshakeable; then, even in deep suffering, you will be comforted. *1 John 4:16*

September 3
Times of need reveal what kind of relationship we have with our heavenly Father. Such periods show whether we have been setting our hope on people and circumstances or whether we have really been trusting in God. Failure to have learnt genuine trust in God the Father makes the hard days harder. Yet it is in these times that the Father calls us back to Himself. It may be His last offer of grace.

Thus it is a decisive moment when we reach the end of our confidence in people and circumstances. Then a door opens for us: repentance. If we repent of our self-sufficiency, acknowledging our sin of separating ourselves from God, we will have access to the Father's love, care and help.

September 4
It is hard for you to come to terms with God's leading. You keep asking, 'Why did this happen to me?' No answer is forthcoming. Yet you would find the answer if you came to God your Father and declared, 'You alone are wise. Your leading is always right. You, O God, love me and will always do what is best for me.' If you pray like this, you are honouring God by admitting that He is right, and whenever God is honoured, Satan, who is sowing doubts in your mind, must yield.

September 5
Love is generous. God, the very essence of love, gives an overflowing measure of all that is good. What can prevent Him? – Only we ourselves. Jesus says, 'Give, and it will be given to you.' But so often we cling to what we have and fail to help others in need and difficulty. Loving us as He does, the Father then has to withhold His gifts from us until He has set us straight again.   *Luke 6:38*

September 6
Do we protest and rebel against the will of God when suffering enters our lives? If so, our relationship with God is like that of a servant, who is indignant when he does not receive what he considers his due. But servants are not children; servants have no share in the inheritance. So stop behaving like a servant. It only makes you unhappy and displeases God. It will cost you your inheritance. Remember, through Jesus' sacrificial death you are called to be a child – a child of the heavenly Father.

September 7

Perhaps at this moment there are things in your life which you would like to wish away – difficult relationships or other unsolved problems causing you distress. Listen! All this is challenging you to use an opportunity you have neglected so far: Turn all your problems into prayer. There is no unanswered prayer. Persevere in prayer until help comes. It will come; indeed, God in His love has already planned how He will help. He is waiting for you to come to Him in prayer.

September 8

When fears, troubles and distress arise, say repeatedly, 'My Lord and my God, "You are my hiding place; you will save me from trouble. I sing aloud of your salvation, because you protect me." ' Then you will find that words of trust spoken to the heavenly Father have power to banish the evil one, who wants to make us afraid and drive us to despair. *Psalm 32:7 GNB*

September 9

You are in great distress, because you cannot sense the presence of God and your relationship with Him seems dead. God is acting as if He were a stranger to you. He seems so far away. You are beginning to doubt His love … Believe that He is showing you His special love now. He wants to make your love pure and genuine. That is why He is testing it.

Love which has stood the test is precious and brings a rich reward. This love proves itself by continuing to trust God in trials and temptations, by obediently walking in His ways, and by making sacrifices for Him. No sacrifice is more precious than that offered in times of spiritual drought. Such love, which is not based on feelings, is the greatest present you can give to the Father.

September 10

God has taken away the person dearest to you – someone who meant everything to you, the joy of your life. You say you cannot live without this person. Hear the Lord saying in your heart, 'I have taken from you someone who is precious to you, so as to give you Someone infinitely greater and dearer: Myself. I want to be your one and all.' Believe this and you will see how Jesus will become the joy of your heart and the source of overflowing life.

September 11

Can we imagine how the heavenly Father must suffer when we so often are a distortion of His image, showing little or nothing of His redeeming grace? We were made in the image of God. The Father would not have given up His only-begotten Son to die on the cross if it were not His ardent desire for us to reflect once again the glory of God. As one saved by Jesus, how great is your desire for His reflection to be seen in your life? Whoever loves God will make holiness his aim, because this is the Father's will for His children. And whoever strives for holiness will attain it, for Jesus redeemed us to this end.

1 Thessalonians 4:3

September 12

God loves us as a Father. He takes care that difficult times are always followed by times of spiritual refreshment. In His love He has already prepared a table for His children in the presence of their enemies and in the face of their troubles. After times of weeping, His children are to rejoice and be glad. So in times of suffering let us look forward to the joyful times which will most definitely follow. Then the oppressive power of sadness will be overcome.   *Psalm 23:5*

September 13

An earthly father who has great influence and power enjoys using it on behalf of his children. How much more so the heavenly Father! By His wonder-working power He wants to pave the way for us on blocked-up roads. He wants to remove the obstacles and make the crooked places straight. He delights in helping us. Yet, sadly enough, He finds few who believe this. That is why few experience it.

September 14

God is saying no to the direction you are moving in. He is stopping you from going any further. What should your reaction be? You, too, should say no. Say to the heavenly Father with a trusting heart, 'I don't want to follow this path if You don't want me to. I want to love only the way You have planned for me. I know that it is the best one, for in Your loving heart You have thought it out especially for me.' Then your troubled heart will be at peace, and you will find that God's leading is best.

September 15

What is a mark of great love? – When a person always wants to have us near him and to share everything with us. This is how God the Father loves us. Though sinful by nature, we are so precious in His sight that He will open the gate to the City of God if we come home as victors. There the Father wants us to dwell with Him for ever. Who can fathom such grace? Live in this attitude of hope. Then all your sorrows will fade away in the light of heaven's glory, and you will be filled with joy and confidence.

September 16
God wants to help His children. However, so often we make ourselves independent of Him. Self-sufficient, we exclude God from our plans and decisions, with the result that we are separated from Him. How, then, can He intervene in our concerns and problems and send help? When we take everything into our own hands, we tie God's hands. Is it any wonder, then, if our problems are not solved?

September 17
God listens to every cry that comes to Him from a human heart. However, many people do not listen for God's answer; they do not really expect any response to their cries. Bogged down with their troubles, they are deaf to everything else. This is why God would appeal to us, 'Listen for My words. In them you will find the answer to your cry for help. Be still, read My Word, and you will hear My voice.'

September 18
In view of the time of testing to come upon the earth, God the Father is now waiting for people who will trust Him implicitly. They are the ones who will experience in peril and hardship that He is faithful, in keeping with His promise: 'I will never fail you nor forsake you.' They will experience His special love and care in the coming time of trouble.   *Hebrews 13:5*

September 19

God, who is love, has an abundance of blessings to impart. He does not want to keep anything for Himself; rather does He want to distribute gifts to His children. He is waiting for us to come with open hands, releasing those things we are clutching. He can place His gifts only into empty hands. How He longs to bless us not just once but time and again! Are we constantly waiting to receive His gifts? Do we keep emptying our hands and stretching them out towards God?

September 20

It is a deep grief to God the Father when He is forced to send judgment upon individuals and nations. However, He has to do so, because we often do not listen to His warnings and do not really want to be freed from our sins. If we could only see the fatherly sorrow of God, we would realize that we frequently bring our suffering upon ourselves because of our hardness of heart. Through repentance, however, we can restrain God's hand. If we are under judgment now, God the Father is calling us to repent and change our ways. When we have a repentant heart, God in His love will turn judgment into grace.

September 21

You complain that God delays sending help. What could be the reason? As your loving Father, God is intentionally leading you into a school of waiting. There He can give you precious gifts: patience, humility, persevering faith. He wants to adorn you with these attributes of Jesus now, so that you may be gloriously arrayed at His throne one day. God wants to give you more than just the help which you are expecting and which will come in

His good time. This is the reason for the long period of waiting and suffering. So thank Him for it.

September 22

God sends you a cross because, as a Father, He has to discipline and refine you. Now He is waiting for your response. Will you respond to the Father like a child? Will He hear you say? – 'I want my cross. It comes from Your hands. You gave it to me, and if You do not want to take it away, I will accept it as a gift from You.' Believe that this act of dedication has power before the invisible world. Satan, who hates the cross, will flee from you, while Jesus, who humbly carried the cross, will draw near to you. Filled with joy, He will take you in His arms. In you He has found a true disciple, one who has obeyed His command: 'If any man would come after me, let him deny himself and take up his cross and follow me.' You have comforted the heart of Jesus and the Father.

Matthew 16:24

September 23

Someone wanting to show us his gratitude might say, 'If there is anything I can do for you, just let me know.' Unbelievably, although we often hurt God, rebel against Him and forsake Him, His Word invites us, 'Let your requests be made known to God.' What tremendous love lies behind this offer! – a loving, fatherly heart which delights in fulfilling His children's wishes. Our heavenly Father encourages us to come to Him with our requests, for He likes giving. Trust in His love, and you will experience the truth of this – provided you live according to His commandments. *Philippians 4:6*

September 24

You say you are too weak and helpless and this is why you cannot believe. The truth is just the opposite. You are still too strong. You have too much faith in yourself. Those who genuinely see their limitations expect nothing of self – but all of God. They are forced to cling to Him for help. That is faith. Desire to be small, weak and needy like a little child. Then you will be able to believe. Then you will receive help from God your Father.

September 25

You are faced with a serious problem, to which there seems no solution. Never seek a hasty and premature solution to your problems. Never seek to know in advance the outcome. It will only cause you anxiety, and you will have yourself to blame. In obedience simply take the next step on the path that lies before you. God will always show you the next stretch of the way and pave it for you. If you proceed like that, things will develop further, and you will see the will of God unfold. Leave the final outcome to God. He is love. The solution, therefore, will always be good, fully answering the questions preying on your mind.

September 26

God the Father is love. That is why He takes such great pains for His children to reflect His love. If, for instance, you have to live with a difficult person, accept this as God's leading for you, His way of working in your life. As your Father, God is now forming His nature of divine love in you. This is something of eternal value. Thank Him for working in your soul. Then you will be helped, and divine love will increasingly be seen in you.

September 27

God the Father always has a tender, loving word for any child of His in need. He says, 'Fear not ... I will help you.' Or He assures him that he is chosen and beloved. From this we have a glimpse of the love in the Father's heart. Whoever opens himself up to this love will be healed of all the troubles in his soul. Feed on this assurance like food, and you will indeed taste how good the Lord is.   *Isaiah 41:10*

September 28

When you think of future calamities, you are anxious and afraid. But even now, while you are feeling afraid, a meeting is being held at God's throne. At God's command His angels are being sent forth to guard you in all your ways – yes, to lift you up in their hands and to carry you through all the terrors to come. Never forget this.

Psalm 91:11-12

September 29

Your heart cries out, 'I don't feel like going on. Things are too hard. It's more than I can take.' But God your Father lovingly says, as it were, 'I am waiting for people who will trust Me in the darkest night and obediently follow My leading, persevering to the end.' Do not turn aside from the path along which God is taking you. Do not abandon it inwardly by grumbling or indulging in self-pity. Such reactions will cost you eternal glory. Instead, thank God your Father for leading you along this particular path in His love, so that one day you may enter the heavenly glory.

September 30

As God's children, we are called to know our heavenly Father personally. This involves becoming sensitive to the sufferings of His fatherly heart, the most wounded heart of all. No other heart suffers so much as His heart, for the greater one's love, the greater one's capacity for suffering. No one can love as much as God the Father, because God is love. So trust Him in everything and give Him glory. That will comfort His suffering heart.

October

October 1

You long to have the Father's approval. You can receive it. In the life of His beloved Son, God has shown us the way. Jesus walked in obedience and gave Himself in serving others. He humbled Himself deeply, identifying with sinners in the River Jordan, drawing from the Father words of approval: 'This is my beloved Son, with whom I am well pleased.' You, too, will have the Father's approval if you show the same attitude of humble obedience and service as did Jesus.

Matthew 3:17; Philippians 2:5-8

October 2

Because God is love, His one thought is to make us happy. But He does not want our happiness to be short-lived; on the contrary, He wants us to have lasting happiness – joy for all eternity. That is why we are not spared His discipline now during this short time on earth. He wants to prepare us for the joy and happiness of a redeemed person in all eternity. The choice is ours: Do we want a short-lived, clouded happiness here on earth, or everlasting, unclouded happiness in the heavenly glory?

October 3

The problems in your life are mounting up. How you will cope, you do not know. Listen to what God would say to you: 'You are not the one who has to cope with these problems. I Myself will deal with them. And no matter how great they are, they cannot be greater than I am. I, your Father, am greater than everything and can deal with the greatest problem. Put your confidence in Me.'

October 4

God is sometimes obliged to judge and discipline us. Who can understand Him at such times? – Only those who have a childlike relationship with God. They recognize the love prompting Him. Children who know what their father's heart is like can see his fatherly love even when he has to be firm and deal with them in ways not to their liking. Our attitude towards the will of God shows clearly how we stand. Those who do not know the Father will react defiantly when they find it hard to accept His incomprehensible will. Do we have a father-child relationship with Him or not?

October 5

You have been wronged. Your heart is wounded. You want your name to be cleared and others to apologize. You keep brooding over the situation. Remember, there is Someone who sees what has been done to you: God, who sees everything. Someone knows what it means to suffer injustice: Jesus. But the Father vindicated Jesus by causing Him to rise in splendour as victor over all His enemies.

The psalmist's words hold good for you too: 'Thou hast maintained my just cause; thou hast sat on the throne giving righteous judgment.' Commit your cause to God. Let Him vindicate you. He will do so, because He is your loving Father, who cares for you. But you have to play your part. Do not try to avenge yourself. Pray that bitterness does not gain room in your heart. 'Love your enemies, do good to those who hate you' is what the

Lord is saying to you. You are to learn to love your enemies.

Psalm 9:4; Luke 6:27

October 6

Your whole life is in a mess. You do not know how to sort things out. Turn to Someone who can. Think of the One who created a wonderful world out of chaos. Is He not able to put right your small life?

Man made in God's image is more precious to Him than the rest of creation. We are His children, whom He wants to help and straighten out. He sent His Son, for He knew what a mess we would make of our lives with our presumptuous self-will, our opposition to His divine laws, and our ready surrender in the face of sin. Now He would say to you, 'Jesus is your Redeemer. He will break your chains, solve your problems and answer your questions. Trust Him completely.'

October 7

You ask, 'How can I hear the voice of God?' Above all, believe that God wants to speak to you. Expect Him to. God loves you. That is why He draws close to you and is near even when you do not feel anything. Be sensitive to the leading of His Spirit when you read the Bible or Christian literature. Consider the words prayerfully. Write down what you experience. Make a note when God's Spirit convicts you, shows you His grace and His promises, or calls you to make an act of dedication. Renounce the things you are bound to and pray in faith. Speak with God about everything, just as a child would speak with his father, or a friend with his friend. God will not only answer – He will do more for you than you could ever ask or imagine!

October 8

You believe in the Lord Jesus Christ. That makes you a child of God, one beloved of the Lord. His beloved have a special claim on His loving care and help. The Father pays special attention to them. Bear this in mind whenever you think of the disasters threatening our world today. Cling to God's promise: 'The beloved of the Lord, he dwells in safety by him; he encompasses him all the day long.' He will protect you as only a father could protect his little one, his beloved child, when in distress.

Deuteronomy 33:12

October 9

God has hidden a gem in every cross and in every suffering He sends you. It is a matter of discovering it. Count on such precious gems, just as a child would expect presents from his father. Believe in the love of God. Then you will discover precious treasures in every cross you bear, and suffering will lose its sting. You will be refreshed and comforted by God.

October 10

When everything in our life and daily affairs runs smoothly, we tend to have little contact with God. So thank Him for difficulties. They are intended to bring us into a deeper relationship with the Father, to draw us to His fatherly heart and to revive our spiritual life. They are the very means of making us happy children of God. So accept difficult times positively and reap their benefits.

October 11

God our Father expects His children to be dedicated to His will in obedience. Indeed, our security and happiness lie in such dedication. Union with the will of God leads to union with His nature, enabling His children to reflect His glory. When God leads you along a path that goes against your will and wishes, He is challenging you to surrender your will to Him. He wants to give you the precious gift of being one with Him.   *2 Corinthians 3:18*

October 12

No longer can you see a way out of your troubles. Count on your heavenly Father, who is the Creator God. In the midst of darkness, distress and confusion, He pronounces day by day His 'Let there be ...' What you regard as impossible now will come about through such a creative word spoken by God. So ask your Father to say, 'Let there be ...'

October 13

The prophet Jeremiah declares that God 'is good to those who wait for him, to the soul that seeks him'. Because the heavenly Father is love, it is His nature to show goodness. Though it might not always seem so at first, everything He sends us is a token of His goodness. Believe that God the Father has your well-being at heart. As a loving Father, God can show His children only kindness. This goes for all His leadings, including His disciplinary measures. Through chastening He brings us release from sin, which not only causes us misery but also keeps us from being happy and secure in His love during the storms of life.   *Lamentations 3:25*

October 14

We worry and fret about things for no good reason. Yet the troubled and fearful could be released from all their cares and worries. They have the privilege of saying

Father to Almighty God. It is a father's duty to provide for his children. Are we making sure that we are children in our relationship with God? Then He will lavish His fatherly care upon us.

October 15

You say, 'So often I have trouble believing.' You cannot believe, because ultimately you expect everything of yourself, or of other people and their help. But now you have exhausted your own resources. That is good. Expect nothing more of yourself. Rely no longer on human aid. Now the time has come when God wants to demonstrate His might and help. By claiming them in faith, you are already helped.

October 16

God is a true Father. A good father pays attention even to the smallest thing his child does. How much more so our Father in heaven! The smallest thing we do in secret – a small sacrifice, an act of kindness – is noted by God. He treasures it in His heart and, one day, will reward us openly when, as the great Rewarder, He gives everyone his reward at the Last Judgment. Should not God's love overwhelm us? He rewards us sinners for the smallest act of love and keeps a record of our tears. Remember this love in the darkest hours. Then your trust will know no bounds, just as God's love knows no bounds.

Matthew 6:4; Psalm 56:8

October 17

Who will be firmly grounded and not swept away when tidal waves of trouble roll across the earth? – Those who have built their lives upon the firm foundation of God's will and His commandments. Those who seek to do the will of God daily, taking His commandments as the standard for their lives, will not fall, even in times of great affliction. They will be firmly established for all eternity.

October 18
Think much about the love of God, your heavenly Father. Then love will gain room in your heart, and you will know that you are surrounded by the love of the Father. Whatever you dwell on in your heart – be it doubts or bitterness or thoughts of love – will gain control over you.

October 19
Jesus once said, 'I do as the Father has commanded me, so that the world may know that I love the Father. Rise, let us go hence.' Jesus did as the Father commanded. In obedience He went to Gethsemane and Calvary and, in so doing, showed the world that He loved the Father. For us, as His disciples, there is only one way to prove our love for our heavenly Father: resolutely taking up our cross and following the path the Father has ordained for us. This is what Jesus is looking for in the lives of His disciples. *John 14:31*

October 20
You are faced with failure. You have struggled unsuccessfully. God in His love always has a way to help you, and that help can also work retrospectively. So sing of victory, especially now in the face of defeat, when you cannot see any evidence of victory. And your defeat will be transformed into victory, for faith can achieve great things, even redeeming the past. Failure can be transformed into victory, because the Father's love is so great.

October 21

You have to follow a difficult path of suffering. You hardly know how you are going to manage. But there is a way. With every bitter step say: 'On paths of suffering, when night surrounds me, I praise Him for the blessing that will come. God's will is goodness and loving-kindness. Good are the ways He leads His own.' Then your heart will be comforted, and out of the night new life will be born.

October 22

A time of unimagined suffering threatens humanity. Even were you to flee to the ends of the earth, there, too, destruction would reach you. The psalmist knew the one hiding-place: 'In the shadow of thy wings I will take refuge, till the storms of destruction pass by.' The covering wings are the mercy of God. Take refuge there with your loved ones. His steadfast mercy will surround you. God is stronger than all other powers, commanding them at will.   *Psalm 57:1*

October 23

'Love Me!' This is the Lord's request to you. You are sad, because you cannot sense any love in you. But love does not show itself merely in feelings. Rather, it shows itself in obedience and in faithful endurance during trials and temptations. By your very steadfastness you can show God that you love Him. Another proof of love is that you always choose God and His way. Do that, and you will be loving God your Father and fulfilling His command. Then He will keep His promise to you. He will love you in return and come and make His home in your heart.

October 24

Be glad that you are weak and helpless. With the power of God – so the Lord tells us – you can accomplish far more than you could by relying upon your own resources, no matter how great they might be. By abiding in Him, drawing upon His strength, you will bring forth more fruit and achieve greater things than you would with your own abilities. So thank Him for making His strength available to you in your weakness.   *John 15:5*

October 25

You are confronted with a mountain of worries. The Lord, however, says it is your own fault that your troubles are overwhelming you. No one has to remain in misery – no one who brings his troubles, worries and needs to the Lord and counts on His help. You will receive help from the Father in so far as you expect and trust Him to give it to you.

October 26

A sign that we have become children of God through our Lord Jesus Christ is that we accept the will of the Almighty as the will of a father. The will of our heavenly Father is always filled with tender, loving care for His children. He never acts like a heartless tyrant. This is the comforting assurance of a child of God even during times of divine judgment.

October 27

You say, 'There's something I've been praying for a lot, but God isn't answering. I might as well give up.' Do not say that. If you are a true child of the heavenly Father, you will keep on knocking and begging. That is a sign of humility. God gives grace to the humble. The Lord listens to humble, childlike prayers.

Sometimes He answers prayer differently than you expect. But He will always listen and, in one way or another, deal with your problem. For instance, He may change your heart, so that you are encouraged and uplifted; then your troubles will no longer depress you. Or it could be that your wishes and desires will become less important to you, and you will not be distressed if they are not fulfilled. Your heart will be at peace.

October 28

Who will be strong and not faint with fear during times of great distress? – Those who have learnt to say lovingly in their hearts, 'My Father, my dearest Father.' Those who now live with a childlike trust in the Father in everyday life, no matter what their needs, will become strong and experience His help when they call upon His name in times of great distress. Practise now going through life in this way with your heavenly Father, calling upon His name trustingly. His name will prove its power and bring you help even in the deepest night of suffering.

October 29

In one of the Psalms God is called 'a very present help in trouble'. And Jesus says to His disciples, 'Lo, I am with you always, to the close of the age.' He is present to help, to comfort, to admonish. Say often during the course of a day, 'Jesus, You are here with me. You will help me!' Then you will experience the Lord blessing you with the help you need, just as He did for those living in biblical times. *Psalm 46:1; Matthew 28:20*

October 30

Does God's heart seem to be closed to you? There is a way to open it – thanksgiving. Thanksgiving is a sign of humble love. The humble are astonished when someone does them even the smallest favour, for they feel undeserving. They respond with loving thanks and try to repay the giver. Start thanking God for even the slightest consideration given by others; note each act of kindness; for ultimately it all comes from His hands. Such thanksgiving will open God's heart wide, and streams of blessing will flow down upon you.

October 31

As a real Father, God chastens and disciplines us. He is motivated by love. Through such measures He spares us much pain not only in eternity but also in this life. Even here on earth we have a foretaste of hell when we live in bitterness, anger, greed and unrestrained desires. God, however, wants us to experience something of heaven and its joy in this life. If we repent and turn from our sins, allowing ourselves to be cleansed, our lives will be changed. Strife will turn to peace, selfishness to love, and we will have a foretaste of heaven.

November

November 1

God can transform shortage into plenty, just as Jesus multiplied the loaves and fish so that there was enough to go round. To this day God can transform a little into a lot – but for whom? In the account of the feeding of the five thousand the disciples were not allowed to eat by themselves the few loaves and fish they had. These had to be shared among the crowds. As they were given away, they were multiplied; and everyone, including the disciples, had as much as he needed. So give, and you will receive. But first place what you have into the hands of God, as the disciples placed the bread into the hands of Jesus. Then the little you give Him lovingly and trustingly will be increased by His blessing. Give in times of hardship as well, and 'the jar of meal shall not be spent, and the cruse of oil shall not fail ...'

Matthew 14:13-21; 1 Kings 17:14

November 2

The parable of the prodigal son tells us something. There is Someone who is interested in you, Someone to whom you are dear and precious, Someone who is looking to see whether you will turn to Him. He is waiting to hear your voice. He is waiting for you to place your hand in His fatherly hand. He wants to help you. Won't you come?

November 3

God is laying a heavy cross upon you. You would like to shake off this crushing load. But did you know that only the proud want to do so? They think they do not need it.

The humble, on the other hand, are well aware that they need chastening. They know how good and beneficial their cross is for them. The choice is yours. Either your cross will oppress you because you refuse to accept it humbly, or else your cross will become light because you praise God for the blessing it will bring you. It is for your own good that the Lord gives you a cross.

November 4

You no longer see any solution to your problems. However, despondency has never changed things; it will not get you anywhere. Trust that God has a solution for you. Trust has always been able to change things.

November 5

Did you pray this morning? Perhaps you think, 'I cannot pray. There is no point in my praying. God does not hear me anyway! I'm too bad.' You are mistaken. God does hear. It is a matter of dialling the right number in order to get through. So begin with the prayer which is preliminary to all other prayers and which never fails to reach God's heart. Confess to Him how weak and sinful you are, where you have failed and done wrong. Tell Him the accumulated sins marring your life. Tell Him what you are like and be honest about your spiritual condition.

Be brave and tell all this to a spiritual counsellor as well. Sin needs to be brought to light and confessed. Then you will receive forgiveness and experience release through Jesus' saving power. God, who loves you, cannot bear to see you unhappy. He is waiting for you to come. All those who confess their sins will be taken into His loving embrace. Their prayers will be answered, because there is no unforgiven sin standing between them and God.

November 6

Times of suffering and chastening are times of preparation. This is why they are not endless. Even here on earth they are followed by times of joy and laughter, which are a foretaste of what is to come. After this life with its times of preparation, there will be everlasting rejoicing and gladness in heaven. Live in expectation of this.

November 7

When are you strong? – When you trust God. But you will be weak when you doubt Him. So be courageous in faith, and obstacles will fall. Think highly of the power and love of God, and you will experience great instances of His help and care. No one who puts his trust in God will be forsaken. *Psalm 9:10*

November 8

You may be tempted to think that it will all be over when a nuclear war breaks out. Then consider this: Even human love always finds a way to help as long as it has the power to do so. God the Father, however, loves you as no human being could; and He has the power to help when no one else can. He always provides a way out of your trials. Keep your eyes open. You may be sure His help will come.

November 9

Blessed are those who in the truest sense of the word have become children of God, children of the heavenly Father through Jesus Christ. They will be spared the anguish that comes from doubting whether the will of God is still love when He has to chasten us and be firm with us. True children of God are sure that, even when their heavenly Father disciplines them, He is motivated by love. They can sense His love in His grief, in the pain occasioned by their sinful behaviour and the need to discipline them. Allow yourself to be humbled, so that you become as small as a child. Then in every chastening you will rest in the Father's will, and His discipline will have a beneficial effect on your life.

November 10

Do you find it hard to believe in God's merciful love? Then consider this: In heaven God will reward us for even the smallest things, although He really does not need to reward us for anything. What would become of us if God were to weigh our actions? Imagine what would happen if He put all our sins and failures onto one scale, and all that we have done for love of Him onto the other. The scale with the sins would be much the heavier. Yet still He rewards us for the smallest cup of cold water we have given to one of our brothers. When we are faced with our sins and failings, this thought helps us to believe that God acts not according to our sins but according to His great mercy.

November 11

You say that God is against you. You cannot do anything right. But it is exactly now that God in His love intends to achieve something great in your life. He wants to put your hip out of joint as He did to Jacob, so that as a pardoned person you may then approach the rising sun, a new and brilliant morning. *Genesis 32:24-31*

November 12

God the Father wants to have His children close to Him. He sends us various troubles and trials in order to draw us back to Himself. But usually we do not welcome these messengers sent to recall us. We grow angry and defiant. And then we wonder why we do not receive the love, gifts and help we expected from the Father. He seems far away.

In every hardship caused by people or circumstances, let us hear the loving voice of God pleading with us to repent. Let us turn to Him with all our hearts. God in His fatherly love longs for us. He wants to have fellowship with us. He wants to make us truly happy in this loving union with Himself. It was for this reason that He created us and Jesus Christ saved us. So welcome the messengers He sends to draw you back to Himself.

November 13

You sense that midnight is drawing near. It is growing darker and darker on earth, with war and persecution of Christians flaring up in various places. Demonic powers are raging across the earth, stirring up sin and lawlessness. Fear grips your heart. But the Lord says to you, 'Be strong, fear not!' By faith the people of God crossed the Red Sea as though on dry land. By faith you, too, will pass through the waves of distress, as though on dry land. By faith you will experience miracles through Him who is 'the same yesterday and today and for ever'.

Isaiah 35:4; Hebrews 13:8

November 14

Do not count on your own strength and ability. They are insufficient anyway. Count on God. His ability and strength will never fail you. In His love and omnipotence He has as much strength and help prepared for you as you need.

November 15

Are you feeling depressed? Are you experiencing trials and temptations? Then the command 'Rejoice always!' is more relevant than ever. Joy needs to be practised, and God challenges us to do just that. He knows that depression and gloom make us weak, and He wants us to be strong. The joy of the Lord is our strength.

So rejoice in the Lord by giving thanks for the fatherly love of God. If He cares for the birds of the air, how much more will He care for you! Thank Him for loving you as His child and for forgiving you for the sake of Jesus' suffering. Then joy will enter your heart – joy that can never be taken from you, because it comes from God, who is eternal. And so you will receive the strength to overcome. *1 Thessalonians 5:16; Nehemiah 8:10*

November 16

God is against the high and mighty who, with their arrogance, stand in the way of God's greatness and His working. So be a child. God the Father is gracious to the small and lowly, drawing close to them. He loves the weak, the helpless, the incompetent. The beloved of the Lord rest in His embrace. May this assurance be enough for you if you are one of the small, weak and lowly.

November 17

We are not at the mercy of militant leaders and powers. We are in the hands of God the Father, who alone can make wars cease. Through fervent prayer, contrition and repentance we can move the hand of God when it is outstretched in judgment. But where are those who avail themselves of this possibility? God the Father is waiting for us to pray and move His heart and hand so that He can be gracious to us and our people again. *Psalm 46:9*

November 18

Perhaps you have prayed to the heavenly Father for something with all the fervour of your heart, and yet He has not answered your prayer. Could there be a hindrance on your part? It cannot be the Father's fault. He enjoys giving His children gifts. But there is a condition to having our prayers answered. We need to have a father-child relationship with God. We need to walk in the way of His commandments and do what is pleasing to Him. If we are obedient, trusting children, God will prove Himself our Father in all things.

November 19

Why does the heavenly Father say so much about rewards? Rewarding is a joyful expression of love. Love always has to give and reward, even when there is not much to reward. Our heavenly Father loves deeply and rewards abundantly. This is why Jesus challenges us as children of our heavenly Father to have the same attitude: 'You, therefore, must be perfect, as your heavenly Father is perfect.'   *Matthew 5:48*

November 20

The love of God the Father is not sentimental. Like a good father, He is firm in dealing with our weaknesses. When we are hardened and stubborn, His love can be like a hammer chiselling us into shape. True love has to be tough at times. It does not rest until the beloved child has become beautiful.

Learn to see the great love of the Father behind all His dealings with you. Then you will find His chastening easy to accept. Do not resist when His hand wants to chisel your stony heart with His instruments, such as people who make life hard for you. When you resist, you obstruct and prolong His work; this leads only to your own harm and disadvantage. Say yes to His chastening. You need it in order to reach the goal He has set for your life. Say yes, and you will enable Him to accomplish His loving purpose for you all the more quickly.

November 21
God's fatherly heart rejoices over a child who says to Him in faith, before seeing the answer to his prayers, 'I know You will help me. Thank You, Father, that I can count on Your help.' Say this, and you can be certain that the Father will not disappoint such trust.

November 22
Doubts fill your mind. You find it hard to believe in the love of God. It was the returning prodigal who recognized the father's heart and believed in his overflowing love. How did this come about? His tears of repentance and confession of sin opened his eyes to see that his father was nothing but love. Similarly, you will come to recognize the loving heart of the heavenly Father if you have a repentant attitude. Repentance will make your doubts disappear.

November 23
Our worrying is a sign that we think we are important. We think that everything depends upon us alone. We think that we are the ones who have to take charge, sort things out and settle all difficulties. However, those who are dependent upon the heavenly Father as true children do not count on their own resources but on the Father's wisdom and power. When we count on Him, our worries will cease.

November 24

God has laid burdens upon you in your personal life and in your ministry. So believe that He will also see to it that you are equipped and strengthened to deal with these burdens. He is not a hard master, demanding without enabling. He has measured your strength and ability. He knows exactly what you need for this situation and has help in mind. But those who in their hearts call Him a hard master will not receive the strength they need, their unbelief, grumbling and defiance having cut off God's help.

November 25

We are being led by the hand of the kindest Father of all. Everything we have and encounter comes ultimately from Him. Whoever has learnt to accept everything as coming from the hand of the Father is at peace, even in hardships and troubles. He knows that, on difficult pathways, the Father is guiding him with a loving hand and sustaining him with a strong arm.

November 26

God leads you into humanly hopeless situations to teach you faith. If you can see how He is going to help you, there is no opportunity for faith. Faith is activated only when no help is in sight. 'Faith is the assurance of things hoped for.' So believe not just once but again and again. Persist in faith, and the day will come when you will see results. *Hebrews 11:1*

November 27

When the thought of the dark times ahead engrosses you, the Lord challenges you not to look at the impending destruction but to look to Him. He does not say, 'I will strengthen those who focus on the horrors in the time of testing ahead.' No, His Word teaches us something different: 'Look unto me, and be saved.' So look to God the Father, who loves you and promises His help and presence in times of affliction.   *Isaiah 45:22 AV*

November 28

Are you discontented? That is not what God wants. God, who loves all His children, wants them to be happy and contented. So He shows us the way to contentment. We embark on that way when we realize the source of our discontent and turn from it. The proverb 'The more you have, the more you want' says it all! The more we want for ourselves, the more dissatisfied we become. That is a spiritual law. But the more we surrender to God in the way of time, energy, love, prestige and rights, the more satisfied we become.

Such is the substance of Jesus' challenge when He says, 'He who loses his life for my sake will find it.' When you start giving up things instead of making demands on God and people, you will experience how God's loving plan for your life is being fulfilled. Do that. Your discontent will yield, and peace and joy will fill your heart.
          Matthew 10:39

November 29

God is the Father of the small and lowly. Through them He performs His greatest works. Desire to be small, and He will use you to accomplish great things.

November 30

Words cannot express what Jesus has gained for us in making us children of God the Father through His sacrifice at Calvary. He has set us free from slavery to legalism, so that we might live like true children, trusting in the Father's love. Whenever someone loves the Father, all legalism, inner tension, narrow-mindedness and joylessness disappear.

Let the Father love you, and love Him in return. Then as a child of God you will be happy. You will be led by His Spirit in all matters. Through such natural, carefree and childlike joy you will draw many others to the Father, for nothing is so compelling as true childlikeness – a happy, cheerful, relaxed personality.

December

December 1
You complain that your Christian life is lacking power and effectiveness. The fault must lie with you. God in His great love is only interested in blessing and empowering us. That is why He sent His beloved Son. He redeemed us to bear fruit and bring blessings to others. He shows us the way.

Begin to make sacrifices for God and His kingdom, sacrifices which cost you something. Offer your sacrifices in faith. When you sacrifice your energy, trust Him to renew your strength. When you sacrifice money and possessions for Him and His kingdom, trust Him to supply your needs in other ways. Then you will experience the love of God as never before, and you will become a channel of blessing for others. *Romans 12:1*

December 2
When suffering is about to get you down, remember that you are not at the mercy of blind fate. Remember, rather, that your suffering comes from the hand of your heavenly Father. Begin to praise God the Father for sending you suffering that will achieve eternal glory. Suffering is meant to make us like Christ and to help us reap a great harvest. So say to the Father, 'I'll suffer gladly. This will prepare me to dwell in glory for ever.' Then blessing and comfort will flow into your heart.

December 3
Perhaps you reckon with God sending help only in so far as this seems reasonably possible. But trust God that He has ways to help you that far surpass your understand-

ing. Reckon with the fact that His power to help is as great as His omnipotence and that He can perform miracles and great deeds beyond human understanding. Then you reckon aright.

December 4

Your life is a storm-tossed ship. You are afraid. You call to God. But the storm grows stronger. The waves are threatening to engulf you. You cry, 'Where is my God? Has He not heard my prayer?' He has! But often His will is to let the storm reach its climax. In allowing this, He has a loving purpose. He wants to draw as much faith as possible from you, in order to present you with the crown of faith one day. In response to your faith, He wants to do miracles today, thus glorifying His holy name.

So when the storm rages and you are shaken, be brave and praise Him, saying, 'Now God is at work. Now great things will happen in my life, and His name will be glorified. I will endure and trust Him.'

December 5

The fact that God is our loving Father means that His will is always goodness. His will comes from a heart full of love. Worship and praise God, recognizing His will as the will of the kindest and most loving Father of all. Continue to worship Him, praising Him for His will, even when He leads you along difficult and incomprehensible ways that are bitter for you. In worship and praise you will find the bitter becomes milder – yes, even sweet.

December 6

Children – not strangers or servants – have access to the treasures of their father's house and to his heart. Do you want to experience this in your relationship with the heavenly Father? Only through faith in your Saviour Jesus Christ can you become a child of God. The cross of Calvary is the gate leading to the Father's house. Bring your sins to the cross in repentance, confessing them before God and man. Then the gate will open and the riches of the Father's house will be yours.

December 7

Fear of the future is depressing you. The Lord would reassure you, 'Have I not told you that I will be with you always? Days of trouble are no exception. On the contrary, then I will be closer to you than ever before. If the hardship is seven times greater, My help will be seven times greater. During the hardest days I will come with even larger numbers of angels to help you. You can rely upon this.' The greater the hardship, the closer God is, and the mightier His help.

December 8

A child of God lives in hope, in a state of expectation. It is natural for him to expect a present from his heavenly Father, something good, some form of help – especially after days of suffering. So be a child. Open wide your heart. And hold out your hands, so that He can fill them with His gifts. With such hopes and expectations you will not be disappointed.

December 9

To love God means to give ourselves fully to Him with our whole life and being, with all our strength, with all our mind. This was the love that compelled Jesus to lay down His life. All true disciples of Jesus, who love God, have the same longing. They are God's true children, and He endows them with power and authority in His kingdom. Just as the sons of a nation give their lives to save their country, so the sons of God give their all to win souls for the Kingdom of God.

Ephesians 5:1-2; Colossians 1:24

December 10
Many people have a personal faith in Jesus Christ and call God their Father. Yet they are unfamiliar with childlike prayer, which God promises to answer. They fail to turn daily from their pride and self-sufficiency, their rebellion against chastening, and their desire for power or prestige. With such an attitude how can they pray in a childlike way and receive God's gifts as true children of His? God gives grace only to the humble. The prayers of the humble and lowly pierce the clouds. Be willing to bear humbling experiences, so that you become a true child. Then your prayers will have power.

December 11
You may think that suffering, trouble and anxiety are the end of the story, but not as far as God is concerned. He has planned release, help, comfort and joy for you. Tell yourself this again and again. Say, 'Thank You, Lord, that help is coming. You have a solution to my problems.' Then your worries will disappear, and you will experience God's help.

December 12
A cross stands high for all to see, and upon it hangs the Son of God. God gave up His dearest and best to such

an agonizing death for our sakes. The cross tells us how much God the Father loves us. It is the guarantee that all His paths of chastening are inspired by love as He seeks to prepare us for heavenly glory. So look at the cross, and you will have a glimpse of God the Father's heart. His love will overwhelm you, and any doubts about His love will disappear.

December 13

Each day brings something different. This day will bring you certain joys and sorrows; the next day, different ones. But nothing happens to you by chance – not even the smallest incident in your life. We read in Scripture, 'As for God, his way is perfect.' God has planned every day of your life, attending to all the details. Everything is perfect.

Learn to see the Father's hand in everything that happens to you. Whatever comes from Him can only be filled with blessing and serve for your good. With a humble, loving and thankful heart accept everything He brings into your life each day, and you will be richly blessed by the love of God – even through events and circumstances that go against the grain.   *Psalm 18:30 AV*

December 14

You are despondent, because you have run out of energy, ability, connections, opportunities – everything that gave you courage and self-confidence. How foolish to despair! There is Someone else to whom you may turn – Someone whose help never fails, whose energy is inexhaustible, and who is always willing and able to help. He is God, your loving Father. Turn to Him in prayer. As your Father, He will listen to your prayers. He will consider them in His heart and, in His wisdom, decide what help to send. The timing will be determined by His love. But He will always help, and you will afterwards acknowledge that He keeps His word – 'Every one who asks receives.'

Matthew 7:8

December 15

You are afraid that God might ask you to make a sacrifice, that He might take something precious from you. This fear consumes you, keeping you from being happy. Put your trust in God. His heart is goodness and love. How could He demand something of you that would ultimately make you unhappy? That is impossible. Give to God of your own free will, trusting implicitly that giving in this spirit will make you strong and happy. God does not accept anything without giving in return. He will reward you abundantly for every sacrifice offered for His sake.

December 16

Your difficulties seem to be so great that you think you cannot cope. They are depressing you. But then there must be something wrong, for God never gives us more than we can bear. You are not seeing things in perspective. Compared with the greatness of God, your predicament is very small – like a grain of sand compared with a huge mountain. No matter how great your problems, doubts and cares, they can never be greater than God in His power and love. Focus on that infinitely greater power and love. Reckon with God – your difficulties will shrink to their proper size, and you will be helped.

December 17

You feel alone and forsaken. You cannot cope with your fears and troubles. The thought of future calamities is more than you can bear. But remember, you have become a child of God the Father through Jesus Christ. Now there is one thing a father cannot do: leave a child on his own to cope with fear and trouble. No true father would do that. And even if such fathers do exist on earth, your heavenly Father will never forsake or fail you.

December 18

A father who loves his child does not like to see anything bad or unpleasant in him. But no father loves his child as much as the heavenly Father loves us. He is untiring in His efforts to make our souls beautiful. Should we not thank Him for the trouble He takes with our upbringing?

When He leads us along paths of suffering, let us renounce all self-pity. Our suffering, which we have usually brought about through our own sin, is not worth the tears – rather should we weep for God's sorrow and the trouble we cause Him. Let us thank our heavenly Father for taking such great pains to bring us up properly, to make us beautiful and happy for all eternity. Then our cross will begin to shine.

December 19

Our heavenly Father wants to give us the greatest gift of all – something that is part of Him – love. He knows that love makes us happy. That is why He has brought it to us through Jesus Christ. We win the hearts of others with love, because people cannot resist love for ever. If we can love, we have peace in our inmost being, even when people are hostile towards us. Love can endure all things. It can be patient and even do good to its enemy. Crucify self-love daily, so that there will be room for the love of God through Jesus Christ in you – and you will have everything.

December 20

Jesus says to us, 'Unless you turn and become like children, you will never enter the kingdom of heaven' – or attain the treasures of heaven through prayer. Let us turn daily from our pride, overconfidence, self-righteousness and all rebellion against God's will and His chastening. Then through prayer we will attain much. Because we are children, the treasures of heaven and the Father's gifts will be ours.   *Matthew 18:3*

December 21

The forces of evil are rampant on earth. It has become dark. But there is Someone watching over us: God the Father. A loving heart, the heart of the Father, assures us of His presence when we are in distress. What more do we need?   *Psalm 91:15*

December 22

'To do you good in the end ...' This was God's intention for the children of Israel during their desert wanderings. To this day He has the same goal in mind for every desert wandering in a person's spiritual life. Keep your eyes on this goal, and you will experience this truth.

Deuteronomy 8:16

December 23

Everything seems hopeless. You can see only obstacles, difficulties, impossibilities. Make use of the lever which can lift and remove all obstacles: the prayer of faith. It is powerful. It can accomplish anything, because the One whom you ask can do everything and wants to use His power for you in your difficulties. If you believe this, you will experience it. When a father sees his child in need, will he not do all he can to help him?

December 24

Rejoice every day like a child looking forward to Christmas. The heavenly Father has lovingly prepared wonderful surprises for you. His greatest gift – the sending of His Son to become our brother – is the guarantee. As a true and loving Father, He has planned only good things for this day and for your whole life. Full of expectation, keep your eyes open for them. Then you will see them. You will be thankful and happy and richly blessed by God's love.

December 25

Rejoice! The Father in heaven has sent the One of whom it is written, 'I have overcome the world.' He has overcome your world, too – everything that is causing you trouble and anxiety. There is Someone who has come to deal with your situation: Jesus Christ. The heavenly Father was thinking of you when He sent His Son. Jesus can deal with the problems in your small world. Bring them to Him, and He will act. You will be amazed at how He is able to solve everything. *John 16:33*

December 26

A servant needs to take care that he receives his due from his master – but not a child. A child naturally has a right to everything in his father's house. In all his troubles, whether of body or soul, he can go to the father. He shares everything that the father has. And if his father is well off, he is well provided for.

But who is as rich as our Father in heaven, who makes us sinners His children through Jesus Christ? Let us take care to be true children of God the Father by loving Him, trusting Him, obeying Him, and depending upon Him. Then we will share in the riches of God and our every need will be supplied.

December 27
As a loving Father, God would like to speak with you, His child. He is waiting for you to come to Him in prayer, to pour out your heart to Him. He is waiting for you to hear what He has to say to you through His Word. You will lose out considerably if you do not take advantage of this opportunity regularly. Only these quiet times spent apart with God, only these conversations of love, can give you the strength to overcome your daily problems. Keep your quiet times faithfully. Fellowship with God is the key to victory.

December 28
Trust, believe, don't throw away your confidence – this is Scripture's repeated message. Believe that God loves you. Believe that He has help for you, a path through the turbulent waters. Trust Him to do everything right, because He is your Father. Yes, trust Him and He will help you. Everything depends on trust. Put your trust in God, who has proved His love by delivering up His Son to redeem us from the depths of hell. Should not your loving Father in heaven also rescue you from your far smaller problems, however hell-like they may seem, be they in daily life or in times of disaster? *Hebrews 10:35*

December 29
Whoever has lived apart from God, with no interest in doing His will, cannot suddenly say one day, 'From now on I want to turn to the Father. Then everything will be all right.' Good intentions will not get us anywhere. If I want to begin a new life of dependence upon the Father,

I must first confess with all my heart, 'Father, I have sinned.' Then through the blood of His Son I will be granted forgiveness and my past sin will be blotted out. I will be cleansed through the blood of Jesus Christ, so that I will no longer live for myself but for God in joyful dependence, in fellowship with Him. Everything in my life will become new.

December 30

God knows how long each one of us will live. The span of our lives is brief, several decades at most. Because God in His love wants to reward you richly one day, He gives you opportunities every day of your life to sow many seeds. Which hours in particular will bring a rich harvest when your life is over? – Those hours which you have dedicated to Him. As a proof of your love, give Him more time. He is waiting for this and will reward you for it – both here and in eternity.

December 31

You are familiar with the practice of bookkeeping in the business world. But now that another year is ending, have you ever thought of balancing the accounts of your personal life? That is, have you straightened out your relationship with God and your fellow beings? One day you will have to account for your whole life. If you have failed to balance the books now, it could be too late when you stand before God's throne. You could come under His wrath and judgment. But let us not forget the loving purposes of God. Scripture says, 'The Lord ... is forbearing toward you, not wishing that any should perish, but that all should reach repentance.'

Today you can still balance the accounts of your life and actions. You can turn from bad ways. You can confess before God and man that which was wrong. You can make amends as far as this is possible. You can show a willingness, even as a forgiven sinner, to accept the consequences of your wrongdoing. You can call upon Jesus to cover the deficits of your life. What an opportunity God is giving you! In His love He cannot bear to see anyone lost. So do not postpone this settlement of accounts. Tomorrow may be too late.   *Galatians 6:7-8; 2 Peter 3:9*

Other literature by M. Basilea Schlink

A FORETASTE OF HEAVEN

(American edition: I FOUND THE KEY TO THE HEART OF GOD) Autobiography, 416 pages, illustrated

'Here I found Jesus, the living God, and not theory. Here I discovered the heart of God, which weeps and laments and overwhelms His children with love. The secrets of a deep relationship of love for Jesus – far surpassing my understanding – captivated my heart and filled me with yearning for a deeper love for Jesus and a closer walk with Him.'

BUILDING A WALL OF PRAYER: AN INTERCESSOR'S HANDBOOK 96 pages

– complete with a song cassette –

When the future of a nation is in the balance, when politics, economics and ethics fail, it is the intercessors who can make a difference. They hold the key to recovery, for they focus on God, from whom alone come blessing and salvation. These texts, songs and prayers, drawn from a selection of Mother Basilea's writings, were born of real-life situations: terrorism, deception, political unrest, lapsed moral standards, natural disasters, spiritual attacks ... Everyone who knows and loves the Lord – not just some spiritual elite – can be an effective intercessor. Here we are told how.

FRAGRANCE OF A LIFE FOR GOD 64 pages

A message for our times when countless offers to escape suffering, especially the cross of sickness, are coming from a wide range of groups (including those campaigning for 'death with dignity'). For everyone trying to discover the purpose of suffering and ways of coping, here is an answer tested amid the trials of everyday life.

I WILL GIVE YOU THE TREASURES OF DARKNESS
48 pages

'This booklet is an excellent spiritual counsellor in print. Whenever depression comes upon me, whenever I have to pass through a time of darkness, here I find where it all comes from and the purpose. There is so much depth to this interpretation. You can sense that it is real and based on personal experience.'

MORE PRECIOUS THAN GOLD 192 pages

A word of comfort, a challenge or a promise for every day of the year. In God's rules for living lies the key to His blessing upon our family, community and nation.

NATURE OUT OF CONTROL? 96 pages

In view of recent floods, fires, earthquakes and blizzards, people are beginning to ask, 'Is God trying to tell us something?' The present age, characterized by turmoil in nature, is an opportunity to know the living God as never before.

PRAYING OUR WAY THROUGH LIFE 48 pages

'This beautiful booklet has already helped me through a difficult time. I have discovered a new way of praying that is making my prayer life stronger.'

REPENTANCE – THE JOY-FILLED LIFE 96 pages

'This book unfolds God's answer to one of the greatest needs in the churches of our time. If you are looking for new life, joy and power for your own spiritual life and for those around you, then this book is a must.'

STRONG IN THE TIME OF TESTING 96 pages

As Christians face growing pressures, the need to prepare for the testing of our faith is even more urgent than when these texts and prayers were originally written. We would never be able to bear the hatred, harassment and persecution in our own strength. Yet, as Mother Basilea encouragingly shares, in Jesus Christ we find all the grace we need to stand the test of suffering.

THE HIDDEN TREASURE IN SUFFERING 96 pages

Cares – Strained Relationships – Fear – Illness – Weariness – Loneliness – Inner Conflict – Personality Problems – Unanswered Prayers – Untalented – Growing Old – Want and Need – Fear of Death – Unfair Treatment – Facing Hatred and Slander ... From the wealth of her personal experience Mother Basilea shares how we can find the treasure that lies hidden in every trial and hardship.

YOURS IS THE VICTORY AND MAJESTY 96 pages

Readers comment: A stirring, dynamic piece of literature. * The insight it gives about future events is something every Christian should know. * How wonderfully the Spirit explains everything to God's children! * The best analysis of the present situation I've come across. Profound, discerning. * Superb orientation for our times.

IN HIM WILL I TRUST 64 pages 20 colour photos
A devotional gift book.

'When I needed some encouragement, I would open any page and be filled with hope and trust.'